THE HOMESELLER'S SURVIVAL GUIDE

Kenneth W. Edwards

Real Estate
Education Company
a division of Dearborn Financial Publishing, Inc.

While a great deal of care has been taken to provide accurate and current information, the ideas, suggestions, general principles and conclusions presented in this text are subject to local, state and federal laws and regulations, court cases and any revisions of same. The reader is thus urged to consult legal counsel regarding any points of law—this publication should not be used as a substitute for competent legal advice.

Acquisitions Editor: Christine E. Litavsky
Managing Editor: Jack Kiburz
Editorial Assistant: Stephanie C. Schmidt
Interior Design: Lucy Jenkins
Cover Design: Salvatore Concialdi

Published by Real Estate Education Company,
a division of Dearborn Financial Publishing, Inc.

Printed in the United States of America

95 96 97 10 9 8 7 6 5 4 3 2 1

Library of Congress Cataloging-in-Publication Data

Edwards, Kenneth W., 1928–
    The homeseller's survival guide / by Kenneth W. Edwards.
        p.   cm.
    Includes bibliographical references and index.
    ISBN 0-7931-1299-0 (pbk.)
    1. House selling.   I. Title.
HD 1379.E343 1995
333.33'83—dc20   94-46255
                                                            CIP

Contents

———————●———————

Preface

———————•———————

In the summer of 1970 my family and I left the pleasant little city of Walnut Creek, California heading toward Montgomery, Alabama for my new assignment with the Air Force. Four years earlier, we had bought our brand new three bedroom, two bath Walnut Creek home (right next to, what else, a walnut orchard) for $30,000 with a no-money-down federal VA loan. It was an easy commute to my job and we enjoyed the quiet, friendly little community we found in Walnut Creek. We enjoyed it even more when we found out how much our home had appreciated in four years. After interviewing several real estate agents, we decided on a price of $43,500. We listed and sold it in one week for full price. It was a stress-free and satisfying transaction with no unpleasant aftershocks.

I will never forget heading out of town on that sunny day in June in our little Volkswagen Bug with a certified check for over $10,000. It's an experience everyone should have—several times, if at all possible. If owning your own home is the American Dream, then selling it trouble-free and profitably is the American Dream fully and blissfully consummated.

My objective in *The Homeseller's Survival Guide* is to provide you with the information you will need to realize that goal when it is time to sell your home, and to help ensure that the whole enterprise doesn't turn into a financial and emotional nightmare. Unfortunately, not all home-selling stories are preordained to have happy endings.

Caveat Vendor

For many years in the homebuying business the operative phrase was "caveat emptor," which simply means "buyer beware." If you bought a home and it turned out later there were a few little incidentals that the seller didn't quite represent accurately, or failed to tell you about, it was likely to be your tough luck. Please understand—that has changed. More and more it has become "caveat vendor," or "seller beware." That's very good advice, and it is critical that you have a good grasp of the entire homeselling process so you know what to be aware of. Even if you hire professionals to represent you in every task related to selling your home, you could ultimately be held responsible for any difficulties that develop.

It Ain't Easy Being a Homeowner

You already know that buying a home is not simple. Selling your home entails the same process, except that instead of shelling out tens of thousands of dollars you are likely to be the delighted recipient of the largest single check you've ever seen.

I hope that all your previous homebuying and homeselling experiences have been free of serious problems and extremely profitable for you. If that is the happy circumstance, at this point you will simply have to take my word for it—the road to that day of rapture when you receive your certified check for more money than you ever expected to have at one time in your life is full of dire threats to your survival.

Your Author's Background and Biases

In my career as an Air Force officer my family and I have bought, sold and rented homes in several parts of this country and overseas. Every homebuying and homeselling experience has turned out extremely well for us. In fact, they turned out so well that when it was time to select a second career after leaving the Air Force, real estate sales seemed like a natural choice. It all looked so easy (it's not). For several years I sold real estate in a small university town in the Pacific Northwest. My wife was also a licensed real estate agent and we worked together as a team. We specialized in residential and small investment properties and were very successful, at least by small town standards.

Organizational changes in the brokerage where I worked prompted me to embark full time upon what had always been my part time passions—writing and teaching. Although I am still a licensed real estate agent and a REALTOR® (not all licensees are REALTORS®), my primary activities now are teaching, writing and consulting—all relating to real estate. Knowing that background you will understand my enthusiasm for the virtues of home ownership. In most circumstances it affords a lifestyle that is superior to other alternatives, and if done right (and with a little luck and a lot of hard work) it can be an incredibly good monetary investment.

You might also assume that as a real estate professional I am going to recommend strongly that when you decide to sell your home you list it with a local broker. I do my very best to be objective on that point. As a consumer I've done it both ways. As a REALTOR® I've seen folks sell on their own and do a great job at it. On the other hand, I've witnessed some monumental disasters. Of course, I've also witnessed some monumental disasters when they listed with a broker. My goal is to be as impartial and unbiased as possible and present the information in a manner that will permit you to make the best decision possible for your circumstance.

You should also know that I do not subscribe to the theory that writing has to be dull to be credible. For that reason I have included a few anecdotes designed to illustrate certain important points and to liven things up and keep them interesting. If you want dull, I've included references to several basic real estate law texts in the bibliography. Please don't operate heavy machinery for several hours after reading one.

Learning To Talk the Talk

Real estate has a language all its own, and it can be quite intimidating to the outsider. I will identify the basic vocabulary you need to be familiar with in order to be an informed homeseller, and define terms in language that is understandable. To help you further, I've compiled a listing of the most helpful books currently on the market that relate to selling your home. As the Book Review Editor for *The Real Estate Professional* magazine, one of the leading national periodicals for working real estate professionals, I get to see just about every real estate book published. The ones I've selected represent the best of the crop.

The Real Estate Profession's Pecking Order

There is frequent confusion in the public's mind concerning the meaning of the terms *real estate agent, real estate licensee, real estate salesperson, real estate broker* and REALTOR®. To get the most out of this book, it's important that you know who's who, and who's responsible for what, so here is a quick rundown.

If you engage in professional real estate activity, which means you are trying to get paid for your services, you must be licensed by the state in which you operate. In most (but not all) states you must successfully complete a series of courses covering the subjects of real estate principles, real estate law and real estate finance. In all states you must pass a written, objective examination.

Those who successfully clear those hurdles become real estate salesperson licensees and work for a real estate broker. It's called "hanging your license." The real estate broker has performed as a salesperson for a mandatory period of time and passed additional testing. All real estate licensees are referred to as agents since they operate in an agency relationship with consumers. I will describe that concept in detail in Chapter 6.

Here's the critical thing for you to remember. The broker is the person who is in charge of and responsible for all operations. You may never see the broker, but that's who is ultimately responsible for everything. Above the broker is a state regulating agency, responsible for administrative, educational and disciplinary matters. It is typically called the Real Estate Commission and I've included a list of those state agencies, along with addresses and phone numbers in the Appendix.

In the United States there are about two million real estate licensees, which includes salespersons and brokers. Of these, roughly 40 percent are REALTORS®. The word REALTOR® is a registered trade name that may only be used by members of state and local real estate boards affiliated with the National Association of REALTORS®. Members must subscribe to the REALTOR® Code of Ethics, a comprehensive document that gets revised frequently to address current issues. NAR also sponsors an extensive educational program for its members and offers a wide variety of professional designations, all of which require additional experience and course work. Just as all soft drinks are not Cokes, not all real estate licensees are REALTORS®.

As a long-time REALTOR® myself I've seen how the organization operates from the inside. While working with a real estate agent who is a REALTOR® will offer you no guarantee of satisfaction, I'm convinced it increases the probability significantly, particularly if you follow my suggestions on how to choose one. You'll see that opinion reflected throughout the book.

Red Flags and Survival Strategies

At the conclusion of most chapters I include a Red Flag Checklist along with recommended Survival Strategies. The term *red flag* simply means this is something that deserves your very close attention.

There's no shortage of examples of red flag items in real estate. For example, if a potential purchaser for your home made an offer contingent upon selling her current home first, that would certainly qualify as a red flag item. You would need to know the possible adverse consequences of such an offer to make your decision on whether or not to accept it. As a matter of fact, that is a red flag item I discuss in Chapter 11. I also use the Red Flag Checklist to amplify and further illustrate certain important points I've made in each chapter, so I encourage you to read them all.

Local Ground Rules

There are significant regional differences in real estate practices. It is important, therefore, to educate yourself not only on the basic home-selling process, but also on local ground rules. You got your first lesson when you bought your current home, but it would be a good idea to avail yourself of all the hometown help you can muster to make certain you are up to date. The best way to do this and to protect your vital interests is to find yourself a competent attorney who specializes in real estate to serve as your advisor. As you will see, I have no problem with people basically going it alone in a real estate transaction, but I recommend in the strongest possible terms that as a minimum you employ an attorney to be your advisor and review and approve any document you sign.

Home prices also differ significantly from region to region, so when we talk specific prices you need to translate everything into the situation as you know it to be in your locality.

Homeselling Facts of Life

If you have sold a home before and all has gone smoothly, don't be lured into a false sense of security. There are several very deep and dangerous pot holes along the road leading to the pot of gold at the end of the rainbow. My job is to point them out to you so you may avoid them and claim your rightful prize.

1

▼

Deciding To Sell

If you are planning to sell your home because your company has just notified you that you are being transferred across the country and you are going to need all the cash from the sale to buy a house at your new location, then your options are limited and your task is clear. You've got to do everything you can to market your home quickly and efficiently. Your goal is to walk away from the whole process with as large a check as possible and with no lingering problems that could come back to haunt you later. If that's your situation, we'll help you achieve your objective.

Alternatives to Selling

If, however, you have some flexibility about when, or even if, you must sell, keep an open mind and consider these possibilities. These options are not ones that would likely get enthusiastic endorsements from real estate agents interested in listing your home, for reasons that will surely become obvious to you.

Stay Put and Upgrade

If you want to sell because you have outgrown your present home, if you simply can't stand the shag carpeting, drippy windows or one-car garage any longer, or if five people using two baths has strained interpersonal relations to the breaking point, remodeling is always a possibility. This would typically be a viable alternative if you absolutely love your neighborhood and can't find another one in which you would prefer to live.

My wife and I recently faced a similar dilemma. Our home is in a tranquil, rural neighborhood on about two acres. From our bedroom window we can watch the deer thin the fruit from our apple trees or prune our rose bushes. However, the house was built in the 1970s, just before builders developed some innovative construction features, such as insulated windows and roofs that don't turn funny colors, mildew, rot and leak in a few years. Every time another major system failed or we collided in our cramped kitchen, we went out house hunting.

Each time we visited a nice home under construction we were dazzled by the bright new colors and the other new features, such as skylights and built-in communications systems. Our problem was that the homes were typically built on postage-stamp-size lots, which meant that instead of seeing deer grazing outside of our bedroom window, we would see our neighbors gazing out their bedroom window. So, after months of house shopping, we decided to remain in our bucolic setting and undertake major remodeling.

This is not a step to be taken lightly. On balance, we think we made the right decision (note that I'm not overselling this option), but let me summarize the lessons we learned from several months of anguish, angst and the most incredible disruption to normal living conditions that I ever experienced, including a year's tour in Vietnam.

• •

Top Ten Suggestions for Surviving a Major Remodeling Project

1. *Get It in Writing.* I don't want to play attorney here, but if you want a contract enforced, it is best to have it in writing with all of the terms explicitly described. At a minimum, you need to clearly specify the work to be performed, the timing, the costs and how payments are to be made. Reputable contractors and other building professionals will provide a written contract as part of the normal process. You should then read it, make certain you understand it and change any item with which you do not agree.

2. *Make Certain That the Proper Permits Are Secured.* This is a dilemma. Not all remodeling projects require permits. It's simpler and easier on you and the contractor not to get one if it's in a gray area. Governmental bureaucrats can move at a snail's pace, impose all sorts of highly debatable requirements upon you and charge you money for the dubious privilege of having worked with them. On the other hand, when it comes time to sell your property, embarrassing questions may be asked about whether or not your nice sun room was built according to code and whether necessary inspections were conducted.

   It's best to err on the side of conservatism, because you will likely be ultimately responsible if a permit was required and you didn't get one. Many contractors will downplay the necessity of getting permits, because it means their work will have to be inspected and approved by a third party, who can often nitpick incredibly. Homeowners also often sympathize with that point of view, because on top of everything else permit information gets shared with the friendly folks who decide how much property tax you must pay. The risks associated with not getting permits when they are required far outweigh the advantages, however.

3. *Check Out Your Contractor and Any Tradespeople You May Hire Very Carefully.* The purported advantage of having a contractor to supervise and coordinate all the work is that it takes the burden off of your shoulders. That's true if you hire the right person. Hire the wrong person and you'll be paying a premium for a deadbeat who causes you more problems than you can imagine. To make certain you get what you pay for, work only with a licensed, bonded and insured contractor.

   Further, it is critical that you ask for references from at least the two most recent jobs the contractor has completed. Call each customer. Ask pointed questions. If you serve as your own contractor, repeat this process with each company you hire and make sure you've got plenty of time to supervise the project on a daily basis.

4. *Find Out Who at the State Level Supervises Construction Contractors and Call To Find Out If There Is a Derogatory File on Your Candidate.* Inquire about the process involved if you have a

problem with your contractor. It would also be worth a check with your local Better Business Bureau. It's a long shot that the contractors will be members, but it's worth a try.

5. *Work with Businesses That Have Been Around for Several Years and, If at All Possible, That Are Local.* When the deck begins to sag a year after it's installed, you want to know that the folks who built it are likely to still be in business and are within a few minutes' drive if you need a face-to-face meeting.

6. *Figure Out Ahead of Time How Much the Job Will Cost and Where You Are Likely To Get the Money.* No matter how carefully you budget, your remodeling job will quite probably cost more than you anticipated. Strange and unexpected problems are sometimes encountered when walls are removed to expose plumbing and wiring from a bygone era. That being the case, you need to line up a reliable and expandable source of money. If you've lived in your home a long time and have a large equity, a "cash out" refinancing will generate funds. Loans given specifically for remodeling are also available. If you get one of these loans, the lending institution will be involved in the venture with you, thereby providing some additional assistance in managing the project.

   Home equity lines of credit are also popular now. They have the added advantage that the interest you pay on them may be deductible from your income tax as mortgage interest. You will likely qualify for that deduction, but the rules are complex, so check with your accountant. Go slow with a home equity loan if you decide to get one. It is a lien against your home, and it's easy to write those checks and build up an eye-popping balance before your realize it. Trust me. We have one. I know.

7. *Dole Out Payments to Contractors and Tradespeople in a Miserly Manner.* Never, never, never make the final payment on any job until it has been completely finished, you have thoroughly inspected it and it meets your (and your mate's, if you have one) total approval. Make sure that last payment is large enough to command the contractor's continued and courteous attention.

8. *Make Certain You Have a System Where Subcontractors and Suppliers Are Paid.* Let's say you hire a contractor to do a total and massive remodeling of your kitchen, including moving a wall or two. The total cost of the job is $30,000 (the price of the first home we bought in 1966). Of that, $15,000 is for custom glass-door cabinets and top of the line countertops. You pay the contractor in installments as the job progresses and then the final payment when the total job is done. But the contractor fails to pay the cabinetmaker. Who is responsible for the debt? You are, bunky. The answer is to make checks payable to both the contractor and the supplier, at least on the major items. Don't feel as though you will insult anyone's integrity by insisting upon this method of payment. It's just good business. You may correctly gather that I've had some firsthand experience on this topic.

9. *Be Ready for Life in the Combat Zone.* You will never again take for granted the comfortable routine of such things as the constant presence of a couple of working commodes. When sawdust permeates everything you own and the smell of paint makes your stomach churn and your eyes water, you will need to be strong. Plan to eat out a lot, keep the windows open as much as possible for fresh air and try to visualize how much nicer your frumpy old homestead is going to look after major cosmetic surgery.

10. *Keep Good Records.* On the bright side, everything you do to your home that qualifies as a capital improvement adds to the cost basis of your home and is an income tax benefit. We'll get into more detail in Chapter 2, but the savings can be substantial. You just need to have the records to prove you did the work. When you eventually decide to sell, you will also want to show your buyer the documentation of all the improvements you made.

• •

Remodeling and staying put for several more blissful years in your serene setting may be the perfect solution for you. But since no one should have to go through two major remodeling jobs in one lifetime, at some point in the future you may still want to put your house on the market and sell it. Therefore, it will be time well spent to stay with us for the remainder of the book.

Keep It and Rent It Out

Every piece of investment counseling I've ever read advises "diversification." After providing for your basic needs, establishing a solid insurance program and amassing enough liquid assets to see you through emergencies, your goal should be to put your investment eggs in several different baskets. Consider the following scenario. If it comes close to describing your situation, I have a suggestion you may wish to ponder.

"Pit Bull" Real Estate Investing

You've lived in your home for several years. It has appreciated considerably in value, and your monthly PITI (principal, interest, taxes and insurance) now represents substantially less of your total income than it did when you originally bought it. As real estate values have escalated in your area, so have rents. You have outgrown your home and plan to sell it and move to a larger place in a newer neighborhood. You expect to realize a tidy profit from the sale but would not absolutely have to have that cash to make a down payment and qualify for financing. Now I realize I have lost many of you with each additional supposition, but stay with me, because if you like the basic premise, you can make adaptations.

What does a pit bull do when it clamps down on an object with its jaws? It hangs on to it with a vise-like grip and, short of death, never lets it go. Why not consider hanging on to your home and becoming a landlord? Here's what this approach has going for it.

"Pit Bull" Investing: The Pros

1. You've Got Great Financing.   When you bought your home, you qualified for the best interest rates and loan terms available because you were an owner-occupant. Banks have this policy because history has shown that owner-occupants are the best credit risks.

However, you probably did not sign any agreement that would let the bank call the loan due if you turned the property into a rental. With the rare exception of some subsidized loan programs, you are completely free to move out of your home and rent it out without changing any of the terms of the original loan.

2. You Know the Product.   You are intimately familiar with the property. Whatever its strengths and weaknesses, you know them. There are not apt to be any big surprises: if the dishwasher is about to qualify for retirement, you won't be shocked when it stops working. One of the real problems with buying a rental is satisfying yourself that it's basically in sound condition and won't turn into a money-eating alligator shortly after you buy it.

3. There Are Income Tax Advantages.   You will be able to treat your home as an investment property, which means substantial income tax advantages. First of all, there's depreciation. That's simply a concept based on the obvious fact that property wears out. Each year you get to deduct a proportionate share of the value of the property from the income it generates. Although what you paid for the property when you bought it, plus improvements, will form the basis from which you may depreciate it (as opposed to its current market value), renting it out will still provide substantial tax benefits, which is especially pleasing to the rental owner: if the anticipated happens, the property will actually appreciate in real value.

4. The Potential for Increased Income Over the Years Is Substantial.   There are some notable exceptions (cities that lost a large military installation or that depended on a single industry that left), but the history of rents in most areas is one of steady increases. When my family rented a house during the Depression, I recall we paid $15 a month. It wasn't a mansion, but it was an entirely adequate little home. When we moved to our current location in 1975, we bought a two-bedroom condo that we rented out. For several years, the rent was $375. Now it is $775, and we're a little under market. Because we got a fixed-rate mortgage, the payment is still $317 per month.

5. The Potential for Increased Equity Is also Great.   Each month your renter pays you, and each month you pay the mortgage. Part of that mortgage payment is applied toward reducing the principal balance owed on your property. At the same time, if property values increase at even a modest amount, your equity further increases. We paid $35,000 for the condo in 1975. Market value now is well over $100,000 (I hope the tax assessor doesn't read this) and our mortgage balance will soon be zero, thanks to some additional payments made against principal.

6. Real Estate Is a Great Hedge Against Inflation. Those of us who have kicked around for a while remember the dizzy days of the 1970s and early 1980s, when inflation went berserk. In times such as those, having a couple of pieces of real property can be a blessing, particularly if it has a positive cash flow (your income exceeds your expenses).

"Pit Bull" Investing: The Cons

1. You've Got To Be Right for the Job. Some people are great at being landlords. Others are just not temperamentally suited for it. If you are a hands-on manager, you could be getting midnight calls about such things as dripping faucets, failing furnaces and commodes that don't flush (yuck). And no matter how good a job you do of tenant selection, eventually you will encounter the renter from hell whose purpose in life seems to be to aggravate you (there must be some left—I couldn't have had them all). Before you launch into your personal property-management career, I advise you to do some research. The most practical and comprehensive book I've seen on the subject is *Landlording,* by Leigh Robinson. It's available in bookstores, is updated frequently, is authoritative and is about as enjoyable to read as a book on real estate can be. Another excellent reference is *The Landlord's Troubleshooter,* by Robert Irwin. Irwin has a great deal of practical personal experience in the field of real estate investment and property management, as can be seen in his writing.

2. Property Values Can Go Down. While it doesn't happen often, it can and it has, and when it does it may be devastating if you are overcommitted. For example, during the go-go 1980s, many real estate speculators got in over their heads buying rental property. They got in with high leverage (not much down) and depended on double-digit inflation to make up for the bloated prices they paid.

When the economy cooled and stabilized, many speculators were left with cash-eating monsters that they couldn't support. This cycle gave rise to the development of what is known as the "subsequent fool" theory, which simply means that no matter how stupid a real estate investment you make, if you can find someone down the road to buy it to at a higher price (the subsequent fool), then all is well. However, when the market goes sour and no one will buy it at any price, you have reached the end game and, sadly, have become the ultimate fool. The moral of the story is that you should always invest in real estate that will be marketable at a profit to prudent investors, either by its inherent quality or by improvements you make in it.

3. There Are Perils.   Being a landlord can entail substantial legal risks. In our litigious society, landlords often make a tempting target. After learning all the appropriate laws, rules and regulations, adequate liability insurance is an absolute must. You should also find and join a local property-management organization and attend as many meetings as possible. These groups concentrate on providing guidance and can steer you clear of some dangerous practices that might otherwise seem quite logical.

4. Stuff Happens.   You've got to be able to come up with cash (sometimes large amounts of it) for emergencies. Prudent real estate investors will earmark part of each month's income for a maintenance and repair fund, that can be as big as several percent of their gross income. The problem arises when something unusual happens, such as a roof you expected to last another 15 years suddenly failing. Such a calamity could result in a bill for several thousand dollars, which would put a severe strain on the typical family's operating budget. Because roofs that repel water are considered essential in laws governing tenant-landlord relations, you would either need to have the cash on hand or have good enough credit to get the work done immediately.

5. Uncle Sam Giveth and Taketh.   If you eventually sell a piece of investment real estate, you could be in for a horrendous income tax hit. You will pay capital gains taxes on your profit, which could be substantial because it's basically the difference between the depreciated value of the property and the price you receive for it. There are creative ways to defer these taxes (mainly by exchanging for more expensive investment property), but the potential for a big tax bill to Uncle Sam is very real. We will get into a few more specifics in Chapter 2.

Running the Numbers

Your individual decision on whether or not to hang on to your home and use it as rental will be determined by your personal circumstances and how the exact numbers work out. Here's a very simplified example.

• •

Investment Analysis: 29 Tranquillity Circle

You purchased your home five years ago. It's a three-bedroom, two-bath ranch style in a modest, well-kept, residential neighborhood with almost entirely owner-occupants. You paid $80,000 for it with a 20 percent down payment and a 30-year fixed mortgage at 10 percent. Your monthly principal, interest, tax and insurance payment is $686. You've had no major problems with the home, and all the major systems and components are in good working order. The home has appreciated in value to approximately $125,000, and you are certain you could rent it for at least $875 per month.

There's a fancy formula that real estate investors use when deciding whether or not to purchase a rental property. At its core, however, it's really very simple. If the income you get for your property exceeds what you have in expenses, you will have a positive cash flow before taxes. When you apply the depreciation schedule, your return after taxes will be even better. In the example of your Tranquillity Circle property, you would likely have a positive cash flow before taxes, even making some pretty conservative assumptions. Of course, your after-tax position would look even stronger. In short, it looks like a money-making proposition for you with great future potential for growth. However, before you make your final decision, it might be a good idea to go over all your actual numbers, assumptions, and best- and worst-case scenarios with your accountant.

• •

Variations on a Theme

As convinced as I am that a rental investment or two (or more) makes good economic sense for those who are temperamentally suited for it, I draw the line at being an absentee landlord. Please note that this is an individual bias and is not a conclusion shared by most other members of the investment advisory community. Typically, they offer what is undoubtedly sound advice: "Go where the numbers are best." If, however, you are moving out of your area and you share my views, you may wish to sell your home and, if the transaction generates sufficient funds, invest some of it in a rental property where you are heading. The downside of this strategy is that it will be more difficult to secure financing and you will pay a premium for it, assuming you can find it. You will also note that when you run the numbers they may not come out quite as well as they did when you analyzed your former home.

If You Must Sell

Because this is, after all, a book on how to sell your home, it is now time, as they say, to grab the bull by the horns and look the problem square in the eye.

Selling Your Home Is a Worthy Challenge

If you have sold a home before, it may have been a smooth process, particularly if you used a competent real estate agent. You may have even come to wonder why you were paying that agent those big bucks for what was apparently a very simple, minimum-effort transaction. Just let me say that there are a lot of things that can go very, very wrong and that if and when they do, you stand to lose a whole lot of your hard-earned money and encounter frustration, stress and anxiety that rank right up there with those caused by life's other major traumas. You have an enormous stake riding on the successful outcome of the entire undertaking. The remainder of the book will identify and describe in detail the threats to your survival, along with strategies to head them off or to overcome them successfully if that's not possible.

Homeselling Strategies

Given the enormous importance of the homeselling venture, it would be wise to go about it with a plan. I will be expanding many of these ideas in detail later, but here's a preview:

Your "Lucky Seven" Homeselling Survival Strategies

1. Get Smart.

Even if you employ consummate professionals to accomplish each and every aspect of selling your home, you need to be well informed about every step in the process. The purpose of this book is to give you a handy and reliable reference in understandable language and in a convenient format. In the event you wish to delve deeper into the sub-ject—and I strongly encourage you to do so—you've got a handy list of good reference books in the bibliography.

2. Cut Your Emotional Ties to Your Home.

This will be tough, but here's what I mean. It is quite common for each of us to become emotionally attached to our homes and our neigh-bors. Under the best of circumstances we would like to sell the place to someone who is going to give it the tender, loving care it deserves. Un-fortunately, I've seen that attitude work to the disadvantage of sellers. I'm counseling you to make your decisions based on hard-headed busi-ness principles. If the potential buyer whom you think would fit in best at your neighborhood's annual Fourth of July picnic happens also to be the best qualified and has made the best offer on your home, wonder-ful. Otherwise, let cold business logic prevail.

3. Assemble a Talented, Dedicated Team.

When I say dedicated, I mean dedicated to you and to your goals. Who should be on your team? In most situations a real estate agent, an attorney, an escrow and title officer (in many areas of the country), and an accountant. Is there one member of the team that is indispensable?

Yes—the attorney. You may be able to get along without a real estate agent, but no matter how knowledgeable you may be, you should always get legal advice from an expert.

4. Know What Motivates Each Participant in the Transaction.

Your attorney gets paid by the hour and is loyal to you. Ditto for your accountant. You know what motivates the buyer—the best house for the best price. How about real estate agents? We will be talking a lot about agency, or who represents whom in a real estate transaction, but please understand one thing clearly up front: Real estate agents get paid when, and if, the transaction closes. No deal, no payday. In most instances, that will work to your advantage, but not always. For example, the agent representing you could advise you to compromise on a point that may not actually be to your advantage simply to keep the buyer happy and the transaction on course to close.

5. Give Yourself as Much Lead Time as Possible.

To achieve the best results, it takes a lot of thought and work to sell a home. The more time you have to plan and prepare, the better off you will be—assuming you use the time wisely. So if you have any control over the situation, do some long-range planning and decision making. If you have to sell in a hurry to get to that new high-paying job in Minot, it can be done, and we'll guide you, but it's far better if you can arrange a little lead time.

6. Keep Good Records.

As you will see when we discuss tax matters in the next chapter, substantial savings are available to homesellers, assuming you know the rules and you can prove your case. Written documentation provides the best—and sometimes the only—acceptable evidence. Even though there will be official records kept of your sale, they will not provide the type of proof you will need to substantiate an income tax benefit. As a minimum, get a large manila envelope and put everything that relates to the sale in it. When you buy your new home, get another large manila envelope and put everything that relates to the purchase in it. At least then you will know that everything you need is in one place.

7. Observe This Maxim: "If It's Not Fair for Everyone in the Transaction, It's Not Fair for Anyone."

No, I'm not being a preachy goody-two-shoes here, and I am not saying that if the buyer makes an offer that's $5000 above your asking price (it does happen), you should shyly defer and accept only what you asked for. What I am saying is that in my long experience as both a consumer and a Realtor® specializing in listing and selling residential properties, the best transactions are those in which everyone achieves their goals. Compromise, yes. Hard bargaining, yes. Aggressive marketing, yes. Creative solutions, yes. Dishonesty, no.

Disgruntled buyers who believe they have been unfairly treated can be grumpy and frequently seek redress in court. When I was studying for my real estate license, we had an instructor whose favorite saying was, "There's only one rule you will ever need to follow when you sell real estate. You will recognize it by its golden color." Original it may not be. Great business advice it is.

2

•••••▼•••••

The Taxing Preliminaries

The friendly folks at the Internal Revenue Service (IRS) are fond of saying that they encourage taxpayers to take advantage of every legitimate deduction and that they do not expect to be paid a cent more than they are lawfully owed. What they don't say is that if you do pay more than you rightfully should have by not claiming a benefit that was legally yours, they will cheerfully keep the money. The primary job of their army of enforcers is not to ferret out overlooked deductions and appear at doors across America with Ed McMahon smiles and certified checks. The operative phrase is "Use it or lose it."

How does this affect you, the homeseller? Consider this scenario:

• •

Profit in Paradise

Five years ago you bought a nice little home on Redwood Drive in the quiet suburban Forest Acres subdivision for $125,000. Since then, you bought lumber and personally built a lovely fence around your spacious backyard, had a hot tub built into your covered rear deck, installed custom wall-to-wall carpeting in the family room and added a garage door opener. Your mate, who is a gardening enthusiast, planted expensive rosebushes, rhododendrons, and fruit and shade trees of every known variety. A couple of years ago the city improved the curbing and sidewalks in your neighborhood and your property was hit with a $3,500 special assessment. You unexpectedly get a fabulous job offer in another part of the state and must sell. You haven't really paid close attention to the real estate market in your local community and are astounded when a REALTOR® you contact to help you establish an asking price informs you that she is convinced you could easily get $165,000 for the house. The spurt in property values resulted in part from the recent announcement that a highly successful electronics firm had committed to building a large campuslike facility in the community.

This would all be great news for both you and various taxing authorities, primarily your state and federal governments, because you will likely be realizing a sizable capital gain, which is taxable. The amount of that taxable gain is what's important to your pocketbook. A variety of things that you did, that were done to you or that you paid to have done may be deducted from the amount. Let's say through ignorance or sloppy bookkeeping you fail to deduct $9,000 from your gain. If the federal government taxes you at the 28 percent rate and the state takes another 5 percent or so (unless you live in one of the handful of states that does not have state income tax) you will needlessly be contributing roughly one-third of that $9,000 to various governments. Don't expect thank-you notes. The key to avoiding these unintended gratuities is knowing the rules and documenting your case. Here's a rundown of the most common situations.

• •

But First, a Few Friendly Words of Caution

Before we get to specific matters relating to taxes and the home-selling process, there are a few important points that need to be emphasized. First, the subject is extremely complex, and your specific situation will require individual analysis. I recommend that if you have not done so before, when it comes time to sell your home, find a professional to offer advice and prepare your returns for you. My personal preference is a Certified Public Accountant with extensive experience in both residential and investment real estate tax matters. It has been my experience that in the long run these professionals will save you money—in some instances a lot of money. Second, even though you hire help, it will be to your advantage to keep up with all the current rules and regulations because it is always safer (and cheaper) to be an informed participant in the process. The rub here is that tax laws have an aggravating habit of changing—sometimes dramatically. So your challenge is to become conversant with the rules as they now exist and then pay close attention to reliable sources of up-to-date information, such as publications from the IRS itself, and reputable financial periodicals. Then, of course, you'll run it all by your accountant. With those caveats clearly in mind, what follows is simply an overview of basic current fundamentals.

Selling Your Home and Taxes: The Basics

To be fair, we have to acknowledge that both federal and state income tax codes encourage home ownership and actually subsidize it through such policies as annual deduction of mortgage interest and a variety of other incentives. Bacause happy homeowners typically make great citizens and end up paying a lot of taxes anyway, there's a very practical reason for such governmental benevolence. Be that as it may, if you play your cards right as a homeseller (and assuming the rules don't change), you may never have to pay taxes on that huge capital gain!

Your Starting Point

Let's say that you do, in fact, sell your little homestead in Forest Acres for $165,000, or $40,000 more than you paid for it. To determine what portion of that is taxable you calculate your adjusted cost basis in the home and then subtract that amount from your net proceeds when you sell. In theory, it's very simple. In practice, it can sometimes get a bit more complex.

Determining Your Adjusted Cost Basis. Adjusted cost basis is a statutory term that describes the figure on which profit from the sale of property is determined. It is calculated by adding certain allowable items (which we will describe) to your purchase price (your original cost basis). Your goal is to get your adjusted cost basis as high and your net proceeds as low as you legitimately may, because you will be subtracting one (the adjusted cost basis) from the other (your net proceeds), and you will owe tax on the remainder. There are two basic methods of adding to the original basis (the purchase price) of your home to reach your adjusted cost basis. You may add (1) certain expenses you incurred when you bought the home and (2) the cost of improvements you made to the property.

Adding to Basis: Homebuying Costs.   These are a few of the most common expenses associated with buying a home, and according to reliable sources I've researched, many are often overlooked by taxpayers searching for ways to add to their basis:

1. Attorney fees

2. Title research and title insurance (often paid by sellers)

3. Escrow fees

4. Recording fees

5. Appraisal costs

6. Property inspection charges

7. Property survey

If you search desperately but can't locate the information you need, you will have to retrace your homebuying steps. When you purchased your home, you were given a bundle of very important documents. One of those papers was what is known as a Uniform Settlement Statement (form HUD-1). Since 1974, federal legislation has required that both buyers and sellers in almost all residential real estate transactions be provided with this standardized form, which contains all the basic financial details regarding the transaction. If you can't locate yours, check with the individual who conducted your closing transaction. Most allowable costs will be reflected here, but not necessarily all of them, because you may have paid for something outside of the close or after the sale closed.

Adding to Basis: Improvements.   If you have something done to your home that increases the property value, adds to its life or adapts it to a new use, then it can likely qualify as an improvement. Putting on a new roof, for example, would be an improvement. Repairing the gutters and downspouts, on the other hand, would be a repair and would be categorized as maintenance. This distinction is important, because you can add improvements to the basis of your home but you cannot add repair or redecoration costs.

There are several areas that homeowners typically overlook when they are recording their improvements. For example, take those rosebushes and plants your spouse bought and added to the landscape. They qualify as an improvement, and over a period of several years can add up. Special assessments also qualify. In our Forest Acres example, you could add the $3,500 you paid for the street and curb assessment (principal only). Of course, there are also gray areas. Painting, for example, would ordinarily be considered maintenance, but if done in conjunction with major reconstruction could qualify as an improvement. Having recently paid for the painting of the whole house (inside and out) I can assure you we are not talking about petty cash here.

Your Next Step: Determining Your Net Proceeds When You Sell. If you've sold a home before, you already know that considerable expense can be involved. Paying for almost all costs can be negotiated between buyer and seller and sometimes even the real estate broker. However, here is a list of some of the more common items for which sellers typically pay and that therefore may be subtracted from gross proceeds of the sale to determine net proceeds.

Homeselling Expenses

1. Attorney's fees

2. Real estate commission. (This is ordinarily the largest single expense. Yes, you can sell yourself and avoid paying a commission. We'll cover that.)

3. Title research and title insurance

4. Closing and settlement charges

5. Transfer tax

6. Inspections

7. Surveys

The Bottom Line: Your Capital Gain

After you get the needed information and complete your calculations, here's what you come up with. To the $125,000 you paid for your home you added both expenses of the buying transaction and the costs of capital improvements during your five years of ownership. That came to $14,000, which you added to your $125,000 purchase price to give you an adjusted cost basis of $139,000. You then added the costs associated with selling, which totaled $11,000 (you used a real estate agent), which, when subtracted from the sales price of $165,000, gave you a net proceed of $154,000. When you subtracted the $139,000 from the $154,000, you arrived at your taxable gain of $15,000.

Now for the $64,000 question. When do you pay the tax? Here's the worst-case scenario. You are under age 55 and you do not intend to buy a replacement home. This one's easy. When the April 15 following the sale rolls around, just fill in your Form 1040, Schedule D, as if your home were any other type of capital asset and pay tax on the gain. Be ready for quite a shock when you get the bill. And don't forget the friendly folks in your state capitol when you fill out that tax return. But now for the good news!

Big Bang Homeseller Tax Break Number One: Deferral

All you need do to defer paying taxes on your $15,000 gain is to purchase a new principal residence (a key concept in this entire discussion) that costs as much or more within two years (before or after, interestingly enough) of the sale of the old one. Considering the importance of this benefit, it's a good idea to know a few more details.

Understand the Vocabulary

Notice that the word defer is used, rather than forgive. Here's how that works. When you get to your new job in your new location you find that it is no challenge at all to find a home that costs a lot more than the one you sold. You settle on a modest ranch-style home for which you pay $175,000. For income tax purposes, your cost basis of the home is $160,000, because you must subtract your deferred gain (the $15,000) from the price of the home. You can repeat the entire sell-buy up process indefinitely, using exactly the same tax accounting procedure. You can readily see that if you did it often enough and if you continued to realize a nice little profit out of each transaction, you would be accumulating quite a hefty tax liability down the road.

Watch the Time Limits

Be aware that the IRS can be very particular about the two-year limit for buying up. Except for some special rules for members of the armed forces or those living abroad when their homes are sold, the IRS expects you to do the deed (buy or build and occupy) within that 24-month period. In one case, the IRS allegedly refused to extend the time limit for a taxpayer who was building a replacement residence that burned down before occupancy. In another instance, the IRS reportedly took a hard line with a taxpayer who became ill and was not able to occupy his replacement residence before the two-year limit expired.

Whether these stories got embellished in the telling or represent actual cases, the word is out among those professionals who advise on tax matters: get it done in 24 months. Remember, you can purchase the replacement residence 24 months before you sell, so you actually have a four-year time frame to work with. The most obvious problem associated with buying before you sell is the challenge of coming up with enough cash.

Know the Rules on What Makes a Home

Understand that anything you may do to alter the principal-residence nature of your home will change the situation. The most common circumstance involves renting part of your home out or having a home office for which you claim deductions. It's not that these activities disqualify your home from the rollover provisions; rather, the part of your home (the percentage) that was used for these purposes will be excluded from the computation and be treated separately as income property, which entails a different set of rules.

Some folks also get hung up on trying to claim a house as a principal residence when in fact they actually spend the majority of their time somewhere else.

Big Bang Homeseller Tax Break Number Two: The $125,000 Exclusion

This is the tax break to which those who are approaching "seasoned citizen" status really look forward. Small wonder. If you qualify, you may exclude $125,000 of any capital gains profit you realized from selling your principal residence. Note that the word is exclusion, not deferral. We are talking big bucks here. If your combined federal and state tax rate is roughly 33 percent, you could be looking at a savings of more than $41,000! That would assume you had built up the entire $125,000 in deferred gains, either in a series of sales or in one or two big ones.

There are two basic requirements necessary to qualify. First, you must be at least 55 years of age when your home is sold. Second, you must have lived in the home for three of the five years prior to the sale. It's wise to make certain you completely understand all of the requirements, for it would be a pity to inadvertently jeopardize such a valuable benefit.

Close Doesn't Count

The IRS considers you to be age 55 from the last moment of the day preceding your birthday. It's not good enough if you hit the magic marker a week or a month after you sell the property. Some folks evidently even believe it's okay as long as they eventually reach 55 in the same calendar year. Not so. And when does the sale occur? It's generally defined as the earlier of these two events: when the deed is delivered or when the buyer takes possession of the property and the responsibilities for it are, from a practical standpoint, assumed. For what could be a $41,000 payday, it would seem to me that it would be extremely prudent to count those days and evaluate those options very carefully and build in a comfortable margin of error.

Marital Harmony

If you are married, what if only one spouse is 55 and fully meets the residency requirements? Here the IRS is a bit flexible, assuming, of course, that you meet rigid standards. You would qualify if you hold the property as joint tenants, as tenants by the entirety or as community property (not tenants in common), and you file a joint tax return. If you do not already know, you may wish to check your deed to see how you hold the property. If there's a problem, your attorney can advise you on possible courses of action to correct it.

Marital Disharmony

The basic rule is that only one lifetime $125,000 exclusion is available to a taxpayer. What that means to a married couple is that neither spouse may have taken advantage of the benefit previously. This requirement leads to some interesting situations. For example, assume you are planning to get married. You and your spouse-to-be both own homes and you both would fully qualify for the $125,000 exclusion. Sell them both before you get married and you each get the benefit, which again could be in the $40,000 range. Wait to sell them until after you are married, and you only get one exclusion. It gets even crazier when one spouse is divorced and used the exclusion in a previous marriage, because that transaction taints the other party, and the benefit is not available to either spouse. Couples contemplating divorce are often counseled to wait until after the split is final to sell their home, because at that point they would both be eligible for the exclusion, assuming neither had used it before. I guess the moral of the story is to spend some time with your accountant and your attorney as well as with your marriage counselor.

How about "Mingles?"

This is a term sometimes used to described unrelated individuals who own property together. If you and another person own a home together and both qualify on all counts (age, residency), then each of you can claim the $125,000 exclusion. That's why divorcing couples who are both qualified for this benefit may be advised to hold off on the legal transfer of the property until after the split.

Ownership and Residency Rules

The basic requirement is that you must have owned and used the property as your principal residence for three out of the past five years. There is actually quite a lot of flexibility built into this provision, so don't assume that your ownership and residency must be continuous and that it must be during the final three years of the five-year period. As long as you satisfy both requirements for 1,095 days (3 x 365) during the 60-month period, you qualify. In addition, there are special liberalized rules for physically or mentally incapacitated persons, and you do not have to meet ownership and residency requirements simultaneously during the five-year period. Run it by your accountant if think you are at all close to qualifying.

Big Bang Homeseller Tax Break Number Three: Being Your Own Banker

In the typical real estate scenario you would put your home on the market and find a buyer, who would visit the local lending institution and secure financing. You would get your money at the close of the transaction, minus any loans and other liens on the property that had to be paid off and other expenses of the sale. At that point, assuming you had a tidy little capital gain, you would either pay your taxes in full or take advantage of any tax code benefit for which you qualified, such as the ones we've discussed. Your situation, however, may not be typical.

• •

Free (and Clear) at Last

You bought your home ten years ago and, based on some advice you read about in a best-selling real estate book, you made additional mortgage payments during that time. As a result, you now own it free and clear. You decide to sell and price it at $150,000. You really do not need all of that cash at one time, so you think it would be a great idea to act as your own banker. You structure a proposed transaction that you think would be attractive to a buyer: 5 percent down, 15-year fixed-rate loan term, at 8 percent, a full point below current mortgage interest rates. No loan fees, no points, no appraisal, no loan application, no credit report, no due-on-sale clause, no sweat. You whip out your handy financial calculator and conclude that for the next 15 years you would receive a monthly check for $1,361, which would amount to close to a cool $250,000 by the time it was paid off. What's not to like about a deal like that?

• •

Let's Talk Taxes

For the moment we will limit our discussion to tax matters. I'll have more to say on the subject of owner financing in Chapter 8. Suffice it to say at this point that there's absolutely nothing not to like about a deal like that—for the buyer.

From an income tax standpoint you are looking at what is termed an installment sale, for which there are specialized rules. If there were not, and if you had to report your entire capital gain in the year of the sale (which you may do if you wish), you could end up paying a whopping tax on what at that point would be nothing but a paper profit. For example, if you had a $50,000 capital gain and paid combined federal and state taxes of 33 percent, you would be facing a $16,500 tax bill. Because you only received $7,500 down, you would have to dig up the remainder elsewhere. Not a pleasant prospect, no matter how good a long-term deal you've struck.

Selling on the Installment Plan

When you receive at least one payment for your property after the close of the taxable year in which the sale occurred, you qualify to report it as an installment sale. The more common situation is similar to the one we described above—several payments over a period of years. Here's the advantage. Instead of paying the whole tax on your gain in the year of the sale, you may spread it over the period during which you receive installment payments. If your contract went the full 15 years, that means you could spread it out over the entire term. By using a standard formula, you would calculate how much of each payment you received represented interest (taxable), how much represented a return of your investment (your cost basis—not taxable) and how much represented your profit on the sale (taxable). You can see that this is not an area for amateurs, so it would be wise to get some professional advice before you proceed.

Landlording

If you decide that you want to enter the esteemed ranks of landlords, you immediately enter life in the fast lane as far as taxes are concerned.

Actually, one of the reasons that investing in rental real estate is so attractive is that there are substantial tax benefits. However, if you think the tax laws as they relate to owner-occupied residential real estate are incomprehensible, wait until you get a gander at the rules as they pertain to rental property. Fortunately for both of us, that topic is beyond the scope of this book, but there are plenty of other volumes on the market that do a good job of explaining the opportunities and the perils—I've listed a couple in the bibliography. The good news is that once you get your tax accounting records for your rental set up properly (we had an accountant do ours), it's a fairly clear-cut operation, assuming you continue to keep good records (and you keep going back to the same accountant). If you keep selecting the right tenants, it can even be somewhat enjoyable.

Help!

When I was starting my real estate career, an old head in the office was fond of saying that it makes about as much sense to do your own taxes as it does to do your own dental work. While I was never tempted to extract any of my own molars, my wife and I did our own taxes for several years. The time period between January (when we made our annual resolution to get organized) and April each year was unmitigated hell.

We finally gave in about ten years ago, got recommendations from people we trusted, and took our tax work to a CPA. We've never regretted the decision. We still keep up with what's going on in the world of taxes, particularly as it relates to real estate, since I teach it and write about it and my wife manages our single rental property. It also remains a lot of work around tax, time since we must sort through all of our bulging manila envelopes and try to create some semblance of order. But it's a monumental relief to be able to dump that pile of papers on someone else's desk. Incredibly, our accountant appears actually to enjoy shuffling through our records, making tidy little piles here and there on his desk, asking probing questions and making notes, and then transforming the whole mess into a neat little package that simply requires our signature. It isn't cheap, but I'm certain that in the long run it has actually saved us money. Just as important, I place a high value on the peace of mind that comes with knowing that our returns have been prepared by someone who actually understands all of that mind-numbing gobbledygook in IRS publications.

Bottom Line

When you became a homeowner, you may have realized the American dream, but you can expect a nightmare or two if you do not become conversant with basic tax matters. When you become a homeseller, it's even more important to know your rights and obligations. My final, friendly suggestion is to study hard and hire good help.

Red Flag Checklist and Survival Strategies

1.   In totaling up the costs of home improvements you made to determine the amount you can add to the basis of your home for tax purposes, you use a conservative minimum-wage hourly rate for the time you contributed to the projects.

Strategy: As unfair as it may seem, you may not count any time you put in on any of the projects. If you hired your cousin Sidney and paid him, you can add it in there, but you are volunteer help.

2.   You own a residential rental property and are planning to sell it, but you first want to locate another one that will cost more because you want to defer your capital gain.

Strategy: Even some experienced investors I know have gotten confused on this point. The tax deferral benefit applies only to principal residences. In other words, you would immediately owe taxes if you sold a rental property for a gain. There is a method of deferring taxes on rental property called tax-deferred exchanges, but that's a whole different story with special (complicated) rules.

3.   You've heard that you may add the cost of landscaping to the cost basis of your home. That's good news for you, since your mate has assembled a particularly large and expensive selection of exotic shrubs and flowers in containers that are displayed on your patio.

Strategy: The cost of landscaping a home is one of the most frequent areas that homeowners forget to include when tallying up their cost basis. However, the potted plants would be classified as personal property (movable) as opposed to real property. They would not qualify unless they were planted and remained as a permanent part of the real property.

4. *Twenty years ago when you bought your home, you had it professionally landscaped with an underground sprinkler system and a wide variety of trees and shrubs. The plants have subsequently matured and are worth a great deal more than they were originally, which leads you to believe they will represent a sizable addition to the cost basis of your home.*

Strategy: Nice try. You must use the original cost of the plants and the labor to plant them. Because the sprinkler system is a permanently installed item, it too may be added.

5. *You've been paying on a $3,500 special assessment the city levied on your property for installing sidewalks and curbs in front of your home. Because the principal has only been reduced by $500 since the work was completed, you assume that is the amount you may add to the basis of your home.*

Strategy: When you sell your home, one of two things must happen to that special assessment: it must either be paid off or the buyer must assume and agree to pay it, if permitted by local authorities (it generally is). It's an improvement that qualifies in full for adding to the cost basis of your home.

6. *Rather than sell your home, you've decided to keep it and rent it out. Because the improvements on the property (the house) are now worth more than $200,000, you anticipate a really nice write-off each month for a depreciation allowance.*

Strategy: Converting a home to a rental is often a cloudy issue. Your original cost when you purchased the home is the starting point for depreciation. In other words, if you've lived in the property for ten years and it has appreciated, you will be using the original cost. It could still be a good deal. Only improvements are depreciable—the land is not.

7. *You are planning to build a new home as your new principal residence to qualify for the tax deferral of capital gains. It will cost a great deal more than the one you sold. Your builder informs you that as long as the*

project is in the foundation stage prior to the expiration of the two-year pe-riod, it qualifies.

Strategy: Wrong. The key phrase is "buy or build and occupy." You must actually occupy your new home within that 24-month time frame.

8.   *You own a nice little vacation home at the beach that you plan to sell. Because you spend more than three months there each year, and because members of your immediate family also spend considerable time there, you feel it could legitimately qualify as your principal residence for income tax purposes. Because you don't plan to sell the family home anytime soon, you see no problem with that idea.*

Strategy: There's a simple little rule the IRS uses that covers this situation: one principal residence per taxpayer. The principal residence is the one in which the taxpayer "principally domiciles." In other words, forget it.

9.   *You sell your home for less than you paid for it. You figure the silver lining is that you will be able to write off part of the loss on your income taxes.*

Strategy: If life were fair, that would be the case. That's not the case. If you make money selling your home, you pay tax on it. If you lose money, you grin and bear it.

10.   *You own a duplex. You live in one side and rent out the other. When you sell it for a large profit, you immediately start looking for a replacement principal residence so you can roll over the gain.*

Strategy: For income tax purposes you have essentially owned two properties. One was a principal residence and one was an investment property. There's a whole different set of rules for each. It won't be simple, so visit your accountant before you make any hasty decisions.

3

·····▼·····

Getting To Know
Your Home

If you were to embark on a career in sales, it would be pounded into your head from the very first day that if you expected to succeed in such a competitive business you would have to get to know your product thoroughly. It would be imperative that you do the homework needed to answer intelligently and honestly any question a customer might ask you.

In selling your home, you've got exactly the same challenge. Whether you do it on your own or enlist the services of a real estate broker to do it for you, it's essential that you know as much as is realistically possible about your one and only product—your home. Further, you will be well served to share that information with your prospective purchasers.

In addition to the marketing edge it will give you, there are a couple of other very important reasons that should motivate you to become intimately familiar with your castle's innermost workings. First, the knowledge will help you to more accurately price it (we'll cover that subject thoroughly in Chapter 7). Second, a growing number of states now require property disclosure, and industry analysts are predicting that all states eventually will mandate some form of property disclosure when a primary residence changes hands.

Even if it is not yet mandatory where you live, I strongly recommend that for your protection you give your buyer a property disclosure statement. There's a practical reason for that recommendation. If you sell your home without disclosing a material fact (commonly defined as any fact that would have a bearing on a consumer's buying decision), and a problem later develops, you could be held liable. Even scarier is fact that if you plead that you were not aware of the problem when you sold the home, courts frequently find that you should have known about it if, in fact, you didn't. That being the case, it makes sense to learn as much as you can and then formally disclose.

So, What's To Know?

If you've owned your home for a while, you may wonder how much there could possibly be to know about it that you are not already aware of. After all, you bought it and have lived in it.

Let me give you a little quiz to test the extent of your knowledge. These questions are based on information that is typically found in state mandatory property disclosure forms. I've relied primarily on Oregon's, because it is one of the most recent, and California's, because it was one of the first and remains one of the most complete. Could you respond to each of these questions in writing and be willing to stand behind your answers?

• •

Quiz: How Well Do You Know Your Home?

Title:

1. Do you have the legal authority to sell the property?

2. Is title to the property subject to:
   - right of first refusal,
   - option,
   - lease or rental agreement, or
   - life estate?

3. Are there any:
   - encroachments, boundary agreements, boundary disputes or recent boundary changes?
   - rights of way, easements or licenses (access limitations) that may affect your interest in the property?
   - written agreements for joint maintenance of an easement or right of way?

- governmental studies, surveys or notices that would affect the property?
- pending or existing assessments against the property?
- zoning violations or nonconforming uses?
- boundary surveys for the property?
- covenants, conditions or restrictions that affect the property?
- lawsuits against the owner that may affect the title?

Water:

Household Water:

1. Is the source of your water:
   - public
   - community
   - private
   - shared?

2. Is there a written agreement for any shared water source?

3. Is there an easement (recorded or unrecorded) for access or maintenance of the water source?

4. Are there any problems with or repairs needed to the water system?

5. Are there any water-treatment systems (including water softeners) for the property, either leased or owned?

6. If the property is on a well, what is the GPM (gallons per minute) flow and has there been a potability test made? Results?

Irrigation:

1. Are there recorded water rights for the property?

2. If water rights exist, have they been used in the past five years?

Outdoor Sprinkler System:

1. Is there an outdoor sprinkling system?

2. If yes, is it operable?

3. If yes, has a backflow valve been installed?

Sewage:

1. Is the property connected to a public sanitary sewer system?

2. If not now connected, is there any sanitary sewer proposed for the property? If yes, what is the timing and what is the anticipated cost to the property?

3. Is the property connected to a septic system or cesspool?

4. If septic or cesspool, when was the date of last service?

5. If septic or cesspool, have there been any problems, such as seepage? Are there any septic or cesspool problems in the immediate surrounding area?

6. Does the sewage system require on-site pumping to another level? If yes, is the pump operative and the system functioning properly?

Insulation:

1. Is there insulation in the
   - ceiling,
   - exterior walls
   - floors?

2. What type of insulation is present in each location?

3. What is the R rating of the insulation in each location?

4. Are windows single pane or double pane?

5. Have the seals on any of the insulated windows broken?

Structural:

1. How old is the roof? What is the composition? Has it leaked? If yes, when, and has it been repaired?

2. Have there been additions, conversions, or remodeling? If yes, type and dates. Were building permits obtained? Was a final inspection made?

3. Are there smoke detectors? If yes, which ones are hard wired?

4. Is there a wood stove? If yes, where? Was it installed with a permit?

5. Has a pest and dry rot, structural, or whole-house inspection been done? If yes, when and by whom? Report available?

6. Are there moisture problems in the home, particularly the basement? If yes, frequency and severity.

7. Is there a sump pump on the property? If yes, where is it located and is it operable?

8. Are there any problems with:
   - interior walls
   - ceilings,
   - floors
   - exterior walls
   - doors
   - windows
   - foundation
   - slab(s)
   - driveways
   - sidewalks
   - other structural components?

   If yes, describe extent and current condition.

Major Systems:

Are these systems in good working order? Describe any problems in detail on a separate sheet.

1. Electrical system, including wiring, switches, outlets and service.

2. Plumbing system, including pipes, faucets, fixtures and toilets.

Fixtures and Components:

Which of the following are included in the sale? For each item, indicate whether or not in good working order. If not, describe.

1. Range 2. Dishwasher 3. Washer/Dryer Hookups 4. Burglar Alarms 5. T.V. Antenna 6. Central Heating 7. Wall/Window Air Conditioning 8. Patio/Decking 9. Sauna 10. Security Gate 11. Water Heater 12. Oven 13. Trash Compactor 14. Window Screens 15. Satellite Dish. 16. Built-In Barbecue 17. Garage Door

Openers 18. Microwave 19. Garbage Disposal 20. Rain Gutters 21. Intercom 22. Evaporator Cooler 23. Gazebo 24. Spa 25. Hot Tub 26. Central Air Conditioning 27. Fire Sprinklers 28. Swimming Pool. 29. Heat pump. 30. Attic Exhaust Fan.

Common Interest:

1. Is there a Homeowners' Association?

2. If yes, what are the periodic monetary assessments?

3. Are there any pending special assessments?

4. Are there any shared common areas, such as walls, fences, pools, tennis courts, walkways or other areas co-owned in undivided interests with others?

5. Does the association carry liability insurance to protect individual property owners from law suits against the association?

General:

1. Are there any settling, soil, standing water or drainage problems on the property or in the immediate area?

2. Does the property contain fill? If yes, where and what type?

3. Has there been material damage to the property or any structure on it from fire, wind, floods, beach movements, earthquake, expansive soils or landslides?

4. Is the property in a designated flood plain?

5. Is the property in a designated slide zone?

6. Are there any substances on the property that would present an environmental hazard, such as (but not limited to) asbestos, formaldehyde, radon gas, lead-based paint, fuel or chemical storage tanks or contaminated soil or water?

7. Are there any underground storage tanks, such as septic, chemical, fuel etc?

8. Has the property ever been used as an illegal drug manufacturing site?

9. Are there any neighborhood noise problems or other nuisances?

10. Are there any notices of abatement or citations against the property?

• •

Getting the Facts

Believe it or not, this list is not exhaustive, but it will give you a pretty good idea about the information you'll need to know about your home to properly disclose material facts. If you've never been faced with the challenge of filling out a form asking this type of information, it can come as quite a shock. Several years ago, when I was actively selling real estate in Oregon (where at the time there was no mandatory property disclosure), I traveled to California to sell my deceased mother's home. When I listed it, the REALTOR® handed me California's lengthy disclosure form and said something like, "This is for you. I'm not permitted to help you. Good luck." Because I had never lived in the home, it was especially daunting.

Individual Research

Your first step in gathering the needed information is to start doing some prodding, probing, testing and inspecting on your own and to document what you find. It would also be a good idea to get all of your basic home records together, including those long-forgotten operating manuals for your furnace, dishwasher and other major components. Many homeowners stop after their personal inspection, but in my opinion that's a serious mistake. First, most of us are not qualified to make some of the required judgments. Second, you can have a formal inspection conducted for a reasonable fee and thereby add a great deal of credibility to the results. Finally, and significant in our litigious society, you can shift much of the responsibility away from you to a professional.

Free Help

Many utility companies offer free consumer service. For example, the gas company may send out a technician to check out your hot-water heater at no cost. Many utilities will do free energy audits, which will give you a pretty good feel for your insulation status along with some tips for plugging up air leaks. If you know you will have to replace a water heater, a local plumbing company may be willing to send someone out to give you an estimate. Don't be afraid to ask other questions while the plumber is there.

Formal Inspections

In the majority of homebuying situations, the normal course of events is still as follows: the purchaser makes an offer on a home contingent on a formal inspection, which the purchaser arranges and pays for. However, in recognition of the tremendous marketing advantage inspections provide, more and more REALTORS® are urging homesellers to schedule them and to use the results either to correct the problems that were uncovered or to disclose them and discount the asking price accordingly.

How much will an inspection cost, and how do you select someone to do it? The fee will depend on the extent of the inspection, but I suggest the blue-plate special: pest, dry rot, radon, asbestos, and all the other items on a standard disclosure form. As you are interviewing prospective inspectors, ask to see their inspection checklist and inquire specifically about its relationship to any state or locally required property disclosures. You could be quoted a price from $200 to $400, lower in some areas and higher in others. If you have a unique piece of property, such as a huge, ancient Victorian with antique electrical and plumbing systems and a mile of subterranean passages, it will cost you more. You will likely also pay a modest extra fee for any additional specific tests. For example, radon is not covered in some basic packages. These extras should not be very expensive.

As is the case when you select other professionals to do work, individual references from satisfied customers whose opinions you respect are the best recommendations. If that's not practical, I'm a great believer in relying on members of reputable professional organizations, who will typically have undergone some type of professional education and subscribe to a code of ethics. One of the most prominent in the inspection ranks is the American Society of Home Inspectors. To become a member, an inspector must submit evidence of having successfully performed a certain number of fee (paid) inspections and then complete a certain prescribed number of continuing-education hours each year. You can get names of members in your local area by writing ASHI, 1735 N. Lynn Street, Suite 950, Arlington, VA 22209. Inspectors who are members of a professional association will make sure you're aware of their affiliation, because it costs them time, effort, and money to belong. Look in the yellow pages under Home Inspection if you are really stumped.

Some states now certify home inspectors, although in most instances it is primarily a registration process with no educational, testing or experience requirements. That is likely to change, because home inspection is a rapidly growing career field and there are abuses. Make certain that the inspector you choose is bonded and also has what is called errors and omissions insurance. In the event a mistake is made, it provides coverage if there's a lawsuit.

It would be extremely wise to accompany the inspector and to ask questions and take notes where appropriate. You will need to exercise judgment here. I am reminded of a sign I once saw in an auto mechanic's shop (I owned a 1978 Chrysler). It read: "Labor charge: $30 an hour. $35 if you watch. $40 if you help." Your objective is to inform and educate yourself, not to grimace each time something is written down and to try to argue the inspector out of listing it. Remember that inspectors go into some pretty grungy places to peek and poke, so it would be wise to have coveralls handy if you're brave enough to slither around on your stomach in a dark, cramped crawl space.

Make certain also that the inspector knows the purpose of the inspection—you will be selling your home and want to know what major problems exist so you can fix or disclose them. The report that is rendered, along with any corrective action that you take, should be made part of the marketing packet that you give to serious prospects.

Fix it and Forget It

As a result of both your own investigation and the formal inspections, you will know a lot about your property—maybe more than you want to know. But if it's bad news, isn't it better to get it at this point rather than when an offer has been made and a transaction is pending?

One of the major reasons real estate transactions fall apart after an offer has been made and accepted is the inevitable haggling that goes on over such things as who is going to pay to have the leaky furnace fixed. Such bargaining can sometimes be headed off by agreeing to a maximum amount for which the seller will pay; if a big ticket item appears, the buyer has the option of backing out. It's so much better to make decisions like this when you don't have a nervous buyer involved.

Armed with the good news and the bad, you have two basic options for dealing with the latter. You can remedy the problem or leave it alone, discount the price accordingly and disclose it to the purchaser. This is not always an easy call, and it will depend on your specific situation and your resources, but from a marketing standpoint it is far preferable to fix it (properly) and forget it.

"As Was" Is Better than "As Is"

It may have occurred to you that you could save yourself a lot of time and effort—and maybe money— if you simply sold your home as is. That's always an option, but there is widespread confusion as to what "as is" really implies. If a homeseller knows of defects that are of a material nature, they must be disclosed. In other words, you could sell it as is, but you would still have to specifically point out material defects. In some states you can actually sign what is known as a disclaimer if you do not wish to fill out a detailed property disclosure, but you are still required to divulge material facts. If you want to pursue this avenue further, you need to make a trip to your attorney.

"Oh No, It's Her Again!"

One of the worst situations an individual in sales can encounter is a customer who knows more about the product than the salesperson. I witnessed that firsthand a couple of years ago when my wife was shopping for a car. She knew exactly the make and model she wanted (top of the line, naturally) along with all of the accessories. The problem was that it was extremely difficult to find the exact combination of model, make, color and accessories all in one car. It was further complicated by the fact that she had to wait a year for the new model, because it incorporated a new feature she really wanted.

That meant we spent months looking at cars, returning to some dealerships several times. She studied all the brochures, read all the magazines, asked questions and test-drove cars repeatedly. When the new model year came out, she knew more about that car than anyone in the state of Oregon. It was sad to see her reduce some otherwise confident and outgoing salesperson to a state of whimpering confusion and ineptitude with her questions. The story does have a happy ending: she found her match in a salesman in our hometown. He knew the product, negotiated a fair price and was able to deliver exactly what she wanted.

Whether it's a real estate agent or a prospective buyer walking through your front door, make absolutely certain you've done your homework and can answer the questions.

Red Flag Checklist and Survival Strategies

1. You ask the home inspector you are considering hiring to recommend a contractor to do the follow-up repair work for problems that are uncovered. "Oh, that won't be necessary," you are told, "we do repair work also."

Strategy: Never hire an inspector who also does repair work, because there is an obvious conflict of interest. If the only reputable inspector in your area does repair work, let it be known clearly before the inspection is made that you will be getting bids and going to another source.

2. You have a home inspection and it turns up more problems than you could have imagined possible. You retrench and take the time necessary to have the major items repaired. The original report looks so bad, however, that you're reluctant to share it with a purchaser.

Strategy: It may be wise to have the inspector do a follow-up inspection (you should be able to negotiate a better price) and issue a new report. Include that one in your marketing packet.

3. The inspector you hire shows up in an immaculate business suit. He informs you that he can tell everything he needs to know about your house without going underneath it.

Strategy: All sorts of wild and crazy things can go on in the crawl space under your house, and the sooner you know about them the better. Better get an inspector willing to do the grunt work.

4. You have an extensive set of conditions, covenants, and restrictions (CC&Rs) that applies to your property. However, the homeowners pretty much ignore them.

Strategy: It would still be essential for you to disclose the existence of the CC&Rs. Let's say one of the restrictions was that no large recreational vehicles could be parked in driveways. The fact that other homeowners were doing that would have no bearing on it being an enforceable restriction. If a concerned homeowner complained, it is likely it would be enforced.

5. You are on a community well with plenty of water generally available. However, during some low-rain years, there are summertime restrictions on the amount of watering that may be done.

Strategy: Just to be safe, I would disclose that. If the new homeowner planted an acre of tomatoes that could not be watered adequately, there might be some unhappiness.

6. There are several towering fir trees along a property line with one of your neighbors. You are not precisely sure which are on your lot and which are on your neighbor's.

Strategy: There's potential for big trouble here. Assume you sell and the new owners decide to cut some of the trees, assuming them to be on their lot. They are not. Whoops. I would strongly suggest a survey to clearly mark the property line.

7. Your next-door neighbor has an old dog that stays outside and barks a lot at night. You've not been able to resolve the situation amicably, but figure Rover can't last much longer anyhow.

Strategy: It would be best to resolve the situation before you put your home on the market, because the dog could qualify as a material fact. Talk to the neighbor again. Talk to other neighbors to see if they share your concern. As a last resort, you may have to complain to local authorities.

8. Your septic system is partly on your property, but the drain field is located on the back portion of a neighboring lot.

Strategy: Step one is to insure that your lot has a recorded easement. It probably does. Step two is to make sure that there are no problems with seepage over the drain field.

9.   *You've heard that if you sell your home yourself and do not use a real estate agent you are relieved of the requirement to give a purchaser a formal property disclosure form.*

Strategy: Although I have not seen all the mandatory property disclosure laws in the country, I strongly suspect that you've heard wrong. A real estate licensee constitutes another element in the equation, but not using one does not relieve an owner of the full requirement of full disclosure of material facts. Run this by your attorney before you go further.

10.   *You've heard that there is a plan to widen the road next to your home, and some surveying has taken place. However, no one has formally notified you of any impending action.*

Strategy: One of my former students got involved in a situation like this in one of her first listings. Bottom line: find out what's going on and disclose.

4

·····▼·····

Selling Your Condo, Co-op, Mobile Home or Home on the Range

If you are about to sell your home and it's a single-family, detached structure on a nice lot located in the city or in suburbia, it's likely that most potential buyers are going to be fairly familiar with the advantages and the challenges of that type of ownership. It's also probable that they and all the other players in the drama—most particularly the lenders—will be reasonably well versed on how the whole system operates. That's not necessarily true if you will be selling a condominium, a cooperative apartment, a mobile home or a rural property.

Although the basic homeselling procedure is the same, and although most of the guidance we provide will apply no matter what type of residence you own, you will have a special challenge if you are selling a home in one of the above categories. For example, in getting to know your product, not only must you be aware of all the standard features we discussed in the previous chapter, but you must also be well versed in all the little nuances that go with owning your particular type of property.

If, as you read the remainder of this chapter, you notice a category that applies to you, you should pay close attention. If you're just reading the information to enhance your general knowledge, you will note that I occasionally use some terms without fully defining them. That's because the people who own the property are already familiar with them. If you would like to get a full treatment of the subject, check the bibliography for some good homebuying book references (there's one called *The Homebuyer's Survival Guide* that comes particularly highly recommended).

Condos

It's obvious that you know all about condo living, because you own one and are considering selling it. You need to understand, however, that many homebuyers have never had any firsthand experience with one and many couldn't even define the word *condominium* for you if they were asked. I know, for I sometimes give my real estate licensing class a little pretest at the beginning of the academic year to determine the depth of their knowledge on basic real estate matters. The percentage of students who can correctly define *condo* has never been impressive.

It would be wise to brush up on your knowledge so you can explain the virtues (and responsibilities) of condo ownership to others. You don't want irate buyers to sue you three months after the transaction closes for failing to disclose something that they thought was a material fact—like that they were limited to one parking spot and that it was located half a block away.

How Well Do You Know Your Condo?

It may have been a while since you bought your unit and all of the details of the transaction may not be fresh in your mind. It's even possible you didn't devour every word on every page of all those documents you received. Here's a rundown on some items you need to check out.

Limitations on Selling.   It's not common, but some condo associations place limits on a condo owner's ability to sell. Some have been known to impose a right of first refusal as a condition. That means that when you decide to put your unit on the market, you must first offer it to the condo association. In other instances—and this might be more common—there is a requirement that you sell only to an owner-occupant. You could not sell to someone who thought they might like to buy the unit as a rental investment. There's actually a very practical reason for that—if a condo development has a high percentage of non-owner-occupants then it will probably be more difficult to get financing on individual resale units. If there is any doubt in your mind about whether there is any fine print that imposes any of these restrictions on you, stop your homeselling enterprise immediately and ferret out the facts.

Limitations on Living.   Rugged individualists are sometimes flabbergasted at the restrictions that are placed on the condo owner. It's also difficult for some to accept the fact that when a decision is made by the condo owners' association, it essentially has the force of law. We own a condo that we've rented out for several years. I'm still smarting from being on the losing end of a debate some time ago with our condo homeowners' association board of directors. In a decision I've yet to comprehend, they decided that individual condo unit owners could put on different styles of roofs (wood or composition) when it was time to reroof. Several of the units in the development are in one-story buildings, so a single building could have as many as four different types of roofing material. Fortunately, the good sense of the individual owners has prevailed and there hasn't been a dramatic difference in contiguous units, but the potential for eye-popping nonconformity exists.

You've come to accept these facts of condo life, and in many instances (assuming rational decisions), they work to the benefit of all and will enhance property values, but it's something you absolutely must disclose in clear and uncertain terms. The best method of refreshing your memory so you can properly disclose is to review the master deed, the condo bylaws and the house rules. In some instances all you will really need are the bylaws, because that's frequently where all of those rules are located.

Get Ready for Your Condo Quiz.   Astute buyers are likely to ask some pointed questions about your condo. Here are a few for which you need to be ready:

1. Is the condo association fiscally fit? What are the monthly association dues and how frequently have they gone up over the past three or four years?

2. Has there been a history of special assessments? If so, for what amounts and for what purposes? Are you paying on any now? Are there any new ones under discussion?

3. What has the history of price appreciation been in the development? What did you pay for your condo when you bought it? What is your property assessed at with local taxing authorities?

(Buyers can ask awfully pointed questions. Of course, you could refuse to answer, but that wouldn't inspire confidence.)

4. What is the proportion of owners to renters in the development? This question is critical, because many lending institutions will not make a loan on a condo if the proportion of owner-occupants is below a certain level, say 80 percent. This could require some digging, but you'll almost certainly need to secure the information.

5. Where do I park? For those who have owned their own homes with two-car garages, long driveways and maybe even a street in front of their house for excess vehicle parking, it can come as quite a shock when they find that they've got perhaps one or two designated parking places. It can come as a bigger shock when they find they can't park their luxurious recreational vehicle on the street in front of their unit. To avoid hard feelings, make certain you locate the part of the bylaws that pertains to parking and point it out.

6. How much freedom would I have to do a little individual gardening? Some condo developments are fairly lenient on this, assuming there are some common areas adjacent to the units that would be appropriate for such use. In other developments it's absolutely verboten and anyone caught with a shovel or hoe rummaging around on the grounds will be severely chastised. This could be an important item for some of your potential purchasers.

7. Who owns the common facilities? The typical arrangement is for the condo owners to own the facilities, but sometimes the developers hang on to them. If that's the case where you live, it would be important to disclose that fact.

8. Are condo owners expected to do any of the association work? In many developments, to keep the cost to the owners down, volunteers handle many routine chores. That owner involvement is actually a good sign in most instances. In the development in which we own a condo, for example, there's a hardy crew of volunteers who do such things as replace burned-out light bulbs in the common areas.

Co-ops

Remember the little quiz I mentioned earlier in which I test my real estate licensing students on their basic knowledge of real estate matters? I have yet to have anyone define co-op accurately. That's not unusual, because outside of a few metropolitan areas, the co-op is largely unknown. I'm not saying this to discourage you, because there are thousands of people who buy them every year, but I just want to remind you to brush up on your basics.

How Well Do You Know Your Co-op?

Again, it would be wise to dig up all the official documents that relate to your purchase of your co-op interests and study them.

Limits on Selling.   I'm certain you are well aware of the restrictions that are placed on selling your stock rights, but you need to get the exact terms clearly in your mind. In most situations the co-op boards are picky, picky, picky about whom they will let into their midst. Although they may not legally discriminate based on such things as race or gender, there are plenty of other legitimate grounds for disapproval, including the feeling that the prospective purchasers may lead lives that could disrupt the peace and harmony of an otherwise serene setting.

Limits on Subletting.   This issue may never have arisen for you, but it could very well be important to a prospective purchaser. If that's a restriction in your co-op (it is in most), then you need to refresh yourself on the precise nature of the limitation.

Limits on Living.   Most co-op boards are thoroughly dedicated to maintaining the tranquil life-styles of their fellow shareholders. You need to review your proprietary lease or occupancy agreement and refamiliarize yourself with the contents. If you are a model citizen, the restrictions may not have struck you as imposing any unreasonable limits on your behavior. Others with less exemplary and more robust life-styles could view it differently.

Get Ready for Your Co-op Quiz.   Here are some questions that a savvy buyer may ask and a savvy seller should be able to answer.

1. How can I get the purchase financed? As you know, this is one of the really difficult nuts to crack for co-op buyers. If your cooperative has solved this problem by affiliating with a lending institution that has agreed to make loans to buyers, then you have an enormous advantage. If not, then you really need to start beating the bushes by asking members of the co-op board and fellow shareholders for recommended financing sources. If you wish to educate yourself on the subject, you can get a free consumer guide brochure on co-op financing by calling 1-800-322-1251 or writing NCB Savings Bank, 139 S. High Street, Hillsboro, OH 45133.

2. Will any portion of my assessment payments to the corporation be tax deductible in the same fashion as home mortgage payments? If your co-op has met certain IRS requirements, then you know that the portion of your payments that goes for real estate taxes and interest on the blanket mortgage are deductible items on your personal income tax statement. You will want to locate the appropriate tax guidance literature and have it handy and ready to share.

3. Is the co-op fiscally fit? If there is a lending institution involved in making loans on your co-op, then they will have set up certain standards that the corporation must meet, including the maintenance of adequate cash reserves for both normal operations and contingencies. Some type of abbreviated cash-flow analysis and corporate operating statement should be available for you to show potential purchasers.

4. How well managed is the co-op? This will be a judgment call and a seller will unquestionably put the best face on the matter, but good management (or poor) will be apparent by not only how well the books balance but also by the physical condition of the property and any amenities associated with it.

5. How have prices of the units held up? This can be an embarrassing question, because there have been some volatile swings in the market value of some co-ops. Hopefully, you live in one where the experience has been more positive, but it's wise to be prepared to face the issue head-on. Of course, there's no money lost

unless someone buys high and sells low, but that's not a great sales pitch. The best argument for buying into a co-op has traditionally been that it is preferable to renting. That's an entirely valid argument and should be emphasized.

Mobile Homes

If you own your mobile home as well as the land under it, then you are aware that for most purposes it is treated as real property rather than personal property. You also know that *manufactured homes* is the preferred term but that most people still refer to them as mobile homes.

How Well Do You Know Your Mobile Home?

Mobile homes are found in a wide variety of locations. If yours is in the country on a small acreage lot, then that presents some special opportunities as well as some unique challenges. If it's in a large development with a homeowners' association, then much of what we've said about condos and co-ops could be pertinent. Your task is to research the situation and become familiar with whatever restrictions may apply.

Get Ready for Your Mobile Home Quiz.   There has been quite a national campaign recently to inform consumers about both the advantages and the perils of mobile-home ownership. Questions like these could surface.

1. When was your mobile home built? Units built after June 14, 1976, are subject to the National Mobile Home Construction and Safety Standards Act. The act sets certain construction standards, so buyers will naturally be interested in when yours was built.

2. Where's your dog tag? That's what some mobile-home owners call the little two-by-four-inch aluminum label that must be placed on the outside rear of each mobile home section and that indicates that the home conforms to federal standards. The plate will also show when the home was manufactured and by whom as well as information on wind and snow loads for the unit.

3. How mobile is your home? In parts of the country where there are frequent tornadoes and hurricanes, the stability of mobile homes has become a matter of grave concern. There are plans in the works to address that problem, but an informed purchaser will likely want to know how well your unit is attached to its foundation. If some shoring up needs to be done, it would be good to have the hatches battened down before you put your home on the market.

4. How hard will it be to get financing? In every area there will be some lenders who specialize in making mobile-home loans. It could be the one with which you have your current loan or it could be a competitor. Mobile homes are eligible for both Federal Housing Administration (FHA) and Department of Veterans Affairs (VA) government-backed loans and many state-level programs. You probably have already learned, however, that getting financing on a mobile home is not quite as routine as it may be for stick-built houses. Lenders will look very hard at collateral, so it would be in your best interests to make certain the mobile home is in inspection order before anyone official (like an appraiser) visits it.

5. Would you carry part of the financing? Of course, this question may be asked of any homeseller, but for some reason it seems to be more frequently a part of a mobile-home sale, perhaps because of the difficulty of getting standard financing for the full amount of the sale. If you are able to handle any portion of the financing, follow these guidelines: get a substantial amount down, do a formal credit check and see a lawyer. You'll find additional guidance on being your own banker in Chapter 8.

Country Homes

If you are what is known in some circles as a gentleperson farmer, then you make your living at a regular job but do some farming as a hobby on your little spread. Selling will involve marketing both a primary residence and a minifarm in one package.

How Well Do You Know Your Farm?

You may be using your land for one purpose, but potential purchasers may have something entirely different in mind. For example, you may be raising beef cattle and have your operation set up that way, while others may view it as a perfect setup for annual row crops.

Get Ready for Your Ranch Quiz.   Here are some possible areas of concern that could prompt inquiries.

1. Can you point out the exact boundaries? An analysis of formal complaints made against real estate agents by buyers reveals that boundary disputes are number one on the list. Even though it's going to cost you some money (quite a lot if you have a large, irregularly shaped property) getting a formal survey is really the only foolproof method of avoiding problems.

2. Can I subdivide the land? That back forty may be the perfect grazing spot for your black angus herd, but a developer may see it as a nifty little subdivision. Much misunderstanding frequently occurs on this issue. In most states it is simply not just a matter of staking off a portion of a larger property and getting a building permit. Find out what the zoning is and what would need to be done to legally subdivide.

3. May I see your water permit? This presumes, of course, that you have one. Water is a critical element in the farming equation, and its availability (or nonavailability) will greatly affect value.

4. What is your soil type? Dirt is dirt, right? Evidently not, because people who know make such a big thing out of finding out its exact composition. If your prospects are thinking of developing their plot into Blueberry Meadows, the dirt has to be right.

5. Who puts out fires around here? A good question. Most rural fire departments are largely volunteer and are not designed to protect residential properties. Point out where the fire facility is located and how to contact them. Fire prevention is a vital topic and should be emphasized to buyers.

6. How much of your farm equipment stays? There is frequently a great deal of personal property used in a farming operation—even a small-scale one. Tractors, mowers, portable fences and irrigation equipment are examples. I know I was dumbfounded when I found out the cost of equipping a forty-acre ranch with water pumps and irrigation pipes. It's best to have an inventory handy.

7. Are there any federal or state tax incentive programs for raising or not raising particular crops? If this has not been a topic of interest to you, check with your local farm agents and other property owners in the area. If there's a land-grant university fairly close, you will also be able to get information there.

Marketing Tips

The more uncommon the home you own, the greater your need for specialized marketing strategies when it's time to sell. Whether you hire a broker or you do the job yourself, you will need to answer this basic question: Who are the most likely buyers for my property? Your challenge then is to plug into that market. Let's take a quick look at each of the categories we've been discussing.

Condos

Look at the residents of a typical condo development and you are likely to see a large percentage of empty nesters who are attracted by the carefree lifestyle. Residents could be young and without children, but more frequently they will be retired or approaching that point in their lives. They like the idea of being able to take off on a three-month trip around the country and not have to worry about the yard being mowed or the weeds being cut.

When my wife and I actively sold real estate, we worked with the local chamber of commerce in responding to inquiries from out-of-towners interested in moving to the area. Many of these individuals were perfectly suited to the condo life-style, and most were extremely well qualified financially, because they had recently sold their homes and were looking for new horizons. It is an extremely rewarding group with which to work. How would you reach these people when selling your condo? The most effective way is to list with a broker who is active in this sort of marketing.

If you sell on your own, you will find that your neighbors in the development are a great source of potential purchasers, particularly if there is a strong feeling of togetherness in your association. For example, over the years we've received inquiries from owners of the condo units adjacent to ours asking if we would be interested in selling. They've had friends who visited them and who were so impressed that they thought they might like to buy in. In any event, make certain you spread the word as widely as possible among other owners in your condo community.

Co-ops

The major motivation for co-op living seems to be financial. Typically, co-ops are most popular where the cost of single-family, detached residential housing is extremely high—so high, in fact, that it is prohibitive for many homebuying hopefuls.

If I owned a co-op, I would first check with other owners and responsible members of the co-op power structure. It is entirely possible that they would have some excellent leads. If it were a buyer's market and there was a scarcity of qualified buyers for units like mine, I would find the best broker I could (one who had sold at least one unit recently in my co-op) and list. I would also learn as much as I could about co-op financing and be ready to offer some owner financing if at all feasible.

Mobile Homes

When you put your mobile home on the market, you will encounter a diverse group of buyers. Many will be motivated by the fact that mobile homes cost less than traditional site-built homes. In some upscale developments, you will get the same type of buyers that are attracted to condos.

If you own a nice piece of rural property, then you'll likely spark interest among people who are looking for a place to build their dream home in the country. In many instances they will plan to live in the mobile home until they are able to build. For that reason, you will be wise to do your homework on what it would take to construct a conventional home on the property. It's also going to be a bit more difficult to get prospective purchasers motivated to come out to look at your spread. You'll want to emphasize the building potential of your property (assuming there is any), because that will be a major draw.

Country Property

I sold two fairly large farms when I was actively selling real estate. The lesson I learned: there's a lot more to know about them than the average residential sales agent is going to know. The one topic that I learned much more about than I really wanted to was water rights. If you have a water permit, make certain it is current and a matter of official record and that there are no impending moves by the state to curtail usage. If there are, you will need to disclose that fact.

If you list, you must locate someone with extensive experience in selling properties like yours. I have a friend in Alabama who specializes in selling farm property. He can tell you all about soil types and land values. If I were in the market to buy a farm or ranch property there, that's who I would contact. That's why it is wise to list with someone with those sorts of credentials if you're selling and you don't plan to solo.

If you don't list, you will need to devote a monumental amount of time, energy and money to bring your property to the attention of qualified buyers. It is possible that you may be able to detect my biases on listing or not listing if you own a farm.

Red Flag Checklist and Survival Strategies

1. Your single-wide mobile home is located on a nice five-acre parcel. When you place it on the market, a couple with six children indicates an interest. They tell you it would be their intent to live in another single-wide as an interim measure and then build a large family home.

Strategy: Their first problem could be with moving another mobile home on the property. It may be permissible, but they better check that out with county authorities. The second problem could be that your septic approval is for a much smaller unit than they are planning. Again, to ensure full and honest disclosure, they should be pointed in the direction of the county officials who approve building permits.

2.   *You own a nice little horse setup just outside the city limits but within the urban growth boundary. Current zoning would not permit horses there. You decide to sell your home, and friends who also own horses are interested.*

Strategy: Your little horse farm may be permitted under a grandfather clause in zoning but would not be allowable for a new owner. That's an important detail you should check out with city and county planners.

3.   *You have a water usage permit from the state for your forty-acre spread on the river but have not actively used it since you discontinued growing seasonal crops several years ago.*

Strategy: Check immediately on state rules regarding the possible loss of water rights for nonuse. Having an active water-rights permit could add thousands of dollars to the value of your property. You may wish to quickly plant a crop of cucumbers.

4.   *You own your proprietary lease in your co-op but have never itemized deductions on your personal tax returns so it really doesn't matter to you whether or not any portion of your monthly assessment is tax deductible.*

Strategy: It could make a huge difference to potential purchasers. It may even be the deciding factor in whether they can qualify for a loan. Get the appropriate information from your co-op board.

5.   *The twenty-acre combination farm and residence that you have on the market is in a governmental tax-deferral program that means you will not pay full property tax as long as the use remains the same.*

Strategy: Some buyers have been hit hard on this. They buy a little acreage and decide to put it to a use different from that of the previous owner. They then discover that by so doing they have triggered back-deferred taxes for which they could be liable. It could be a very large sum of money. They naturally go after the seller for not disclosing fully. The only viable alternative is to make certain you know the rules and that you disclose them in writing.

6.   You've heard talk in your condo development about a possible special assessment of several thousand dollars to upgrade the swimming pool area. No final decision has been made, so there is no information on what the amount of the assessment would be per owner.

Strategy: This could be a gray area. Should you disclose this information to a prospective purchaser? My advice? Find out the best case–worst case scenario and disclose both.

7.   There is a prohibition against selling to non-owner-occupants in your condo development. The market is slow and you locate a couple who would like to take the property on a lease with an option to purchase.

Strategy: It is possible that this would not be considered a rental because a purchase option is involved. However, it would be prudent to seek specific approval from the condo board of directors for the arrangement because you don't want to take your home off the market, have people move in and then find that you are in violation of the owner-occupants only rule.

8.   One member of your co-op's governing board has made it clear that he would much prefer it if you did not attempt to sell your unit to a member of a minority racial group.

Strategy: Co-op boards have a great deal of discretionary power in approving potential shareholders in the corporation. However, they must abide by both the letter and the intent of federal, state and local fair-housing laws. Discriminating based on race is prohibited by federal law and the penalties for violating the statute can be severe— particularly when there's a corporation involved. You need to clear the air on this issue immediately with no equivocations. You could also get in serious trouble.

9.   Your mobile home is on a hill in a quiet rural setting. The lower portion of the thirty-acre property seems to be under water most of the year but it does not interfere with access from the main road to your property.

Strategy: Can we say "wetlands?" If the people who bought your home were doing so with the hope of constructing a site-built home, they could be hindered in their plans if your property has a wetlands designation or is under consideration for one. Check with your county planning staff, find out the actual status and if appropriate disclose to prospective purchasers.

10.   You've located a buyer for your ten-acre ranch home with a projected close date of June 30. It's now May and you have a five-acre plot of alfalfa hay that will be ready to cut in August. You plan to return to harvest it and sell it to the owner of a local horse farm.

Strategy: You can see that this could cause problems. The standard arrangement would be for you to include in the sales agreement the right to reenter the property and harvest your crop. If there were nothing in writing and the buyers assumed they were purchasing that about-to-be-harvested crop along with the real property, you've got the basis for a nice little dispute. Make it clear who gets to bale the hay.

5

·····▼·····

Polishing the Palace

Suppose for a moment that your lifelong dream has been to own a 1957 Ford Thunderbird. It's not an obsession, so you're not willing to sacrifice little Egbert's college fund to achieve your goal, but you dutifully check out ads in the paper. Your spouse is not quite as enthusiastic as you are about the venture but has agreed to ride with you occasionally if you find one the family budget can afford. One morning you see this notice on your company bulletin board: "Vintage 1957 Ford Thunderbird. Original owner. Fulfill your fantasy. 77 Happy Days Lane. Cruise on by."

You excitedly call your mate to share the good news, and on your lunch hour you head out on your own to go car shopping. When you locate the address you see the object of your affection in the driveway. At least you think it's a '57 Thunderbird. It's hard to tell because of the thick layers of grime, and it's difficult to concentrate because of the wild-eyed poodle yapping at your feet. Two of the tires are almost flat and the others are paper-thin. The car windows are open and the smell of baby diapers badly in need of washing mixes with what you conclude to be evidence of the poodle having marked his territory. There's a large pile of assorted tools on the backseat and floor.

The owner, Bubba Buttstomper, is on hand to ask you if you would like a test drive. You reluctantly agree, so Bubba gets the jumper cables out and gives the dead battery a quick boost. In addition to not being able to take a deep breath, the ride is marred by violent rocking and rolling courtesy of the original-equipment shock absorbers and of the poodle, who has taken a liking to you and is enjoying the trip in your lap. The smoke from Bubba's cigar doesn't help matters. When the nightmare is over and you finally get home you sadly announce to your spouse: "Sorry, but I'm going to have to keep looking."

The foregoing, of course, is fictitious and strains credibility. In real life, when people sell their cars, they wash them, polish them, clear out the debris, steam clean the engine, get them tuned up, paint over any little dings, buy a few low-ticket replacement items like batteries, tires and shocks, and plug up any holes that conduct fumes from the engine to the passenger compartment. When you test-drive, it will be along the smoothest roads in the neighborhood, and the family pet will definitely not accompany you. What's difficult to understand, particularly considering the value of the asset, is why so many people do not put the same effort into getting their homes ready for public inspection when selling them.

Survival of the Fittest

It will help you achieve and maintain the proper perspective if you remind yourself that when you decide to sell your home it is going to be in a fierce win-or-lose competition with other properties for those coveted ready, willing and able buyers. Every year in the United States, millions of previously owned homes are put on the market. Happily, most sell. Unhappily, many do not—in some years as many as 20 to 30 percent. In some places and at some times the percentage is higher than that—a lot higher. It's difficult for most of us to imagine that it would be possible to offer our home for sale and get no takers. We, after all, bought it and have lived happily in it for years. But it does happen.

Proper pricing is the number-one factor that will sell a home—and we'll get to that—but packaging the product to its best advantage is also critical. It's also a major reason that some homes command a premium price. In most instances, the comparatively modest amount of money you will spend to spruce things up will be more than offset by the return you will realize from a successful sale.

Where You've Been—Where You're Going

It would be useful at this point to quickly recap where you are in your homeselling quest. (1) You've decided not to remodel and you don't fancy yourself a landlord, so you will definitely be selling. (2) You are intimately familiar with all the appropriate federal and state income tax rules pertaining to real estate, but just in case, you have your trusty accountant standing by to answer any tough questions (like "What should I do now?"). (3) You've thoroughly inspected your home from top to bottom, inside and out, looking for serious structural and mechanical flaws, and have made copious notes. (4) You've had a professional inspection done, including pest and dry rot, radon and asbestos. You accompanied the inspector and have a copy of the formal report. (5) You've compiled a complete file of all pertinent house records, including utility payments for the past year. You've got a wealth of information and a plan of action to correct deficiencies. Now what you want to do can best be described by the phrase, "And now it's showtime!"

Through the Eyes of the Buyer

Because you are vitally interested in how prospective buyers will view your home, do the best job you can of mentally shifting gears and putting yourself in their shoes. Specifically, here's what I suggest.

Scope It Out

Spend some time driving around your neighborhood, including the most likely routes to your home. You've seen the sights a thousand times and probably don't pay much attention anymore, but most buyers will be seeing them for the first time. There's not a lot you can do if the only road to your home goes by a working rock quarry, but if there are several routes and one is a great deal more scenic than the others, that will logically be the one you recommend to people who ask for directions.

Map It Out

Get a city or county map and use it to prepare your own map of how to get to your home. Include hospitals, shopping, schools, libraries, parks, recreational facilities, public transportation and anything else that might interest a prospective buyer. Indicate the distance to each from your home. You will want to have this reproduced and put in your informational packet for prospective purchasers. If you list with a REALTOR® you can ask for help on this one.

The Good Neighbor Policy

Think back to when there was a home in your immediate neighborhood on the market. If you were paying close attention, here is what you would have noticed. As people drove by the house with the For Sale sign in front of it, they slowed down and looked at it closely. When they got by it they probably continued to drive slowly and looked at all the nearby homes.

If the people were seriously considering the home, I can assure you they would have studied their prospective immediate neighbors intently. They may have even stopped, knocked on some doors, and asked a few friendly but pointed questions about the quality of life there. In addition to the apparent pride of ownership displayed by the homeowners in the neighborhood, one of the deciding factors in our purchasing our current home was the enthusiastic "You'll love it here!" response we got from a lady down the street upon whose door we knocked. The day we moved in, her daughter arrived with a large plate of "welcome to the neighborhood" cookies.

If, on the other hand, your next-door neighbor's property badly needs major cleaning you've got a problem. You may have learned to live with it and it may no longer bother you much, but it will be a big negative for a buyer. The more lead time you have to encourage the neighbors to tidy up, the better. Because you (or someone you hire) will be spending time in your yard getting things shipshape, that would present the best opportunity to broach the subject of a joint effort. Offer help, if that would be appropriate. If you do not have good rapport with your neighbors, find out who in the neighborhood does and try to solicit their help. If you have a neighborhood association, work diplomatically through it. Improvements will enhance the value of everyone's property.

Home, Sweet Home

You've cruised the surrounding area and the immediate environs and you've looked at everything as though it were for the first time. It was easy to be critical of others, but now for the real challenge.

Visualize that For Sale sign in your front yard, take a deep breath and get mean.

Park your car across the street from your property, get out and look at your house from that vantagepoint and through fresh eyes. When you and the inspector went through, you were looking for meat-and-potato items. Now you're looking for things that will help you "sell the sizzle," as they say in the advertising business. Starting with your first step into your front yard and continuing to the drain in the basement, decide what needs to be done to improve appearances. Armed with a no-nonsense attitude and a pencil and a pad to take notes, you will be on your nit-picking way.

Curb Appeal. Looking from across the street, you discover it's hard to view your home. The assorted varieties of fir and pine trees that looked so great when you bought the house have attained awesome maturity. The dense shade has caused the lawn to thin out and surrender to a moss invasion. What started as little rosebushes, azaleas and rhododendrons were planted much too close together and are crowding each other out. Some plants have died. *Recommendation:* Get your chain saw sharpened or hire tree trimmers. Let the sunlight in and open up the view. We had a similar situation at our home caused by a large grove of oak trees in our front yard. They were beyond my capability to trim, so I hired a group of daredevils who called themselves arborists. They put on the most spectacular display of high-wire artistry I've ever seen, all the while carrying idling chain saws strapped to their belts. The end result bordered on miraculous. We can now see our home from the road again and it helped the atmosphere inside the house dramatically because of the increased sunlight (on those rare occasions in Oregon when the sun shines).

Down the Lane. As you walk down the blacktop driveway past your recreation vehicle and boat toward the house, you notice cracks, holes and oil stains that you had somehow previously overlooked, as well as a healthy growth of ivy that has escaped its boundaries and is intruding onto the driveway surface. *Recommendations:* First, you need to find a temporary home for the recreation vehicle and boat. As impressive and nice as they may be, you are not trying to sell them, and they will give a cluttered and crowded impression and obscure the view of your home. You may be able to park them at a friend's house temporarily (a very good friend), or you may need to rent space for them.

Next, you should get the ivy trimmed back and keep it back. If it has found its resourceful way up the side of your house, get it off. Then check on getting the blacktop driveway resealed. If it's a cement drive-way, it will require a different treatment by a pro, but it must be taken care of. We have an aggregate cement front walkway that had built up an impressive deposit of dirt, scum and moss over the years. I had little success in cleaning it until I found a miniature hose nozzle that pro-duces a very fine, forceful stream of water, which effectively cleans those little crevices.

You will also need to thin out overplanted shrubs and remove dead and dying ones. Some you can transplant, others will have to be rele-gated to the mulch pile, as dreadfully hard as that will be for those dedicated gardeners among you. Homeowners almost invariably over-plant when landscaping, even when they hire pros. It's hard not to make that mistake, because during the early years the appearance is enhanced by the numerous and vigorous young plants. Get bark chips or other mulch to cover in the newly opened space.

Through the Front Door.   I'm afraid I'm going to have to take over now. It's just simply too painful for most of us to be as detached and objective (and occasionally heartless) as we need to be to get the living space in our homes ready for potential buyers to see. I'll offer suggestions that may, or may not, apply to your situation.

Barb Schwarz is a dynamo out of the Seattle, Washington, area whose background is in interior decoration, education and real estate. Among many other ventures, she has produced a consumer video enti-tled *How to Prepare Your Home for Sale—So It Sells!* It does such a good job that it won a national consumer award from a professional real estate education organization when it was first released. I've relied heavily upon it to prepare these remarks, and I've included it in the bibliography if you're interested in ordering it. Or you may suggest to one of your local real estate brokerages that they order it and make it available to prospective customers (after you see it).

Schwarz's guiding philosophy in preparing a home (or staging it, as she refers to it) is that "the way we live in a home and the way we sell a home are two entirely different things." Keep that in mind as we pro-ceed through the following checklist.

• •

Show and Sell Homeseller's Checklist

1. *Entry area.* This will be the first interior space that your prospects see, so it should be clean, light and free of clutter. Because it's a high-traffic area, it is not at all unusual to find chipped tiles or scratched wood on the floor. Those things need to be corrected, and it would probably be good to get new floor mats for both outside the front door and the entryway. If the light fixture is dirty or does not project well, clean it or get another one.

2. *Kitchen.* When people look at homes, they invariably spend a great deal of their time looking at the kitchen. In many households, it is the center of activity, and it therefore gets checked out thoroughly. Getting it in inspection order will present a special challenge, because you will continue to use it several times a day and you will want things like the coffee maker, mixer, can opener and bread machine out and at the ready.

   "Clear the decks" should be your operational mandate. Your goal should be to have the countertops as free of objects and as clean as possible. If you only use the bread machine once a week, find a place for it out of sight. Ditto with the mixer and anything else you can possibly relegate to an inner sanctum somewhere.

   Speaking of inner sanctums, you've got a major job awaiting you inside your kitchen cabinets. You've probably got much too much stuff there, some of which you rarely use, unless of course, you are the Felix Unger type in which case you may go straight to the next chapter. While you're in there, it would be good to scout around for any little food deposits that may have inadvertently gotten dropped. They could invite little four-legged night visitors who have a disgusting habit of leaving their calling cards.

3. *Living room, dining room, family room.* Now we're ready for the real test. These are the rooms that we really live in and have adapted to be comfortable and homey. But remember the Schwarz dictum: "The way we live in a home and the way we sell a home are two entirely different things." Start by looking

at each piece of furniture. Do you really need it? You would be stunned at how eliminating a chair here and a table there opens up a room and makes it look much larger.

Next, survey the walls. Are they cluttered with an assortment of pictures, paintings and plaques? What may have a real sentimental value to you could be another person's eyesore. For example, for years we had a large Venetian painting on our wall. We got it when we were living in Italy, and it was an original. To us it looked great, probably because of its sentimental value. To others it likely looked garish. If there's any question about the tastefulness of an object, take it down.

4. *Bedrooms.* Everything we've said about the other living areas applies to the bedrooms, along with one big addition—closets. If I were to leave my computer right now and walk upstairs to our master bedroom closet and open the door I would be greeted by a bulging array of clothes hung so tight that it is impossible to see any of the back wall. At least that's the way it is on my side of the closet. Your goal should be to arrange all of your closets so they look like my wife's side—neat, tidy, and room for your clothes to breathe.

5. *Bathrooms.* For obvious reasons, the emphasis here must be on cleanliness and sanitation. If there are several people in your clan, including members of the male species, you've got to get everyone trained to observe minimal rules of social decorum. An air freshener in each bathroom would also be a good idea. It would also be wise to keep fresh, light-colored towels on the racks and to keep the window cracked slightly if it's an outside bath and it's not 20° below zero outside.

6. *Outside decks.* Decks have a bad habit of not aging gracefully. If yours are spotty, mildewed and weathered, you should consider having them stained or painted. In some instances, they may require cleaning or sanding first. If you have deck furniture, arrange it neatly and get rid of anything that's really ratty. Many of us stack our firewood on the deck. That's a big no-no, because little critters that crawl and eat wood frequently take up residence there. Firewood should be moved away from the house.

7. *Attics and basements.* The two things that these areas have in common are that we rarely go there and that we typically fill them with assorted oddments. Buyers will go there—or should—to take a look. When they do, what they should see are orderly and uncramped spaces.

8. *Pungent pets.* Another Schwarzism is, "If we can smell it, we can't sell it." If you've allowed Rover and Tabby full access to your home and they've occasionally had an accident on your carpet, you're either going to have to do a major cleanup yourself or call in professional carpet cleaners. Although I'm reluctant to put smokers in the same category with pungent pets, your concerns are basically the same. Tobacco smoke lingers and it will absolutely turn off anyone who does not smoke (and many who do) who looks at your home. It would be good business to establish the inside of your home as a smoke-free environment, at least while you are showing it

• •

The Mother of All Garage Sales

You would be absolutely amazed at what people will buy at a garage sale. A couple of years ago we had a major one when we were getting a rental ready to occupy. Things I thought I would have a tough time getting the Salvation Army to accept as a donation were pounced upon by eager buyers waiting in line when we opened the garage door. On the other hand, a few items I thought people would fight over remained unsold. There's a knack to holding a successful garage sale. Cruise around on the weekends and see how the pros do it. You are likely going to be attempting to dispose of a lot of merchandise, so it makes sense to try to make some money out of it to help defray some of your other costs.

How about Offering a Home Warranty?

You may be so impressed with your efforts in getting your product ready for the market that you would be willing to personally warrant it against defects. That won't be necessary, and it wouldn't be advisable either. There are, however, companies that will do it for you. The question is whether it is a good marketing strategy and whether it would be worth the cost to you.

Warranties on resale homes have become very popular, particularly in places like California. Real estate agents love warranties because they take a little of the potential heat in case something goes kaput shortly after the buyers move in. Some brokers like warranties so much that they pay for them themselves as a listing incentive. Sellers like them because they offer some insulation from aggravated buyers and they make homes more marketable. Buyers like them because they feel as though they are protected against unforseen potential disasters.

In actuality there are a lot of exceptions and large deductibles, but that's not germane right now. Offering a warranty should increase the value of your home, at least in the amount you pay for it, and will likely help sell your home faster. A policy for the first year would probably run between $300 and $400. You can get names of local companies who offer warranties by contacting inspection companies, escrow and title companies, attorneys who specialize in real estate or real estate brokers. If I were putting my home on the market now, I would go for the warranty.

Show Time!

After you've done the best job you know how on getting your home ready for market, it would be a good idea to invite some fresh eyes over to get their opinions on what else might be done—or undone. One of your remaining major decisions will be to determine how much to ask for your home. If you follow my suggestion you will have several REALTORS® over to take a look and to get their pricing input. That goes even if you decide sell on your own. That would provide a perfect opportunity to solicit suggestions for further home showing improvement.

Red Flag Checklist and Survival Strategies

1.   Your 80-year-old grandfather lives with you and has his own room. He's politically active and politically incorrect. Several of the signs on his wall would likely anger members of other political persuasions.

Strategy: The conventional wisdom in this situation is that anything at all that could possibly offend should be removed from the house before showing. After all, you want the focus of attention on your home, not the 1948 election. You might tell him that you want to help him start packing for the impending move. Good luck.

2.   *You've thinned out the plants around your home and it looks a great deal better, but many of them still crowd up a little against the house itself.*

Strategy: You need to trim all plants and branches away from the house so there is no contact at all. That includes the roof, which can present a special challenge. In deciding how much to trim away from the sides, assume you will have a house painter (you may) who must have access to all surfaces.

3.   *Your furnace has worked perfectly for 13 years, so you conclude there's no need to put it through a test run before you put your home on the market in July.*

Strategy: It may work perfectly, but we're talking sight, sound and smell here. What if the neighbor's long-lost pet gerbil had found its way into your heating duct and couldn't find its way out? If a prospect turned the system on just to see how it functioned, the smell could be interesting. Better run it through its paces in private, July or not.

4.   *Your kitchen cabinets are from another time and place. You hear an ad on the radio about a method of replacing the cabinet doors that is substantially cheaper than installing new cabinets.*

Strategy: This situation represents something of a dilemma, and your decision would depend on the condition of your cabinets. The cost of a total replacement will stagger your mind, but even a refacing is not inexpensive. It's a judgment call, but cleaning and perhaps repainting might be your best alternative.

5.   *You hear what sounds like a squirrel racing around on your roof, but you can't be sure that it's not coming from your attic.*

Strategy: Evidence of the occasional presence of little creatures such as squirrels and mice sometimes eludes even the sharp eye of a home inspector. A mouse racing around inside your wall can sound like a teenage skateboarder going at full tilt, and there's no assurance that he won't decide to scamper just as a potential buyer is ready to sign the full-price offer to purchase. If you keep hearing the suspicious sounds, you would be wise to call in a professional exterminator to help out.

6. *The red shag carpeting in your den is in great shape, but you're not certain other folks would share your enthusiasm for the color or style.*

Strategy: The general rule of thumb in a situation such as this would be to leave it and let the new owners replace it with a carpet of their own choosing if they so desire. However, shag carpeting (red and purple varieties, in particular) seems to repulse some people so thoroughly that I would be tempted to replace it with a neutral color, high-wear carpet.

7. *You have every copy of* National Geographic *for the past ten years. The most recent issues are on your coffee table in the living room, while the remainder are neatly tucked away in the adjacent bookshelf.*

Strategy: Unless they have some value as a collector's item, you may wish to thin your collection. Regardless, you need to clear coffee tables of all but a couple of tasteful items and empty bookshelves so they do not look too crowded.

8. *As you clean your house and decide which pieces of furniture and other items it would be good to temporarily get out of sight, give away or sell, everything seems to end up in the garage. It's so bad you can't get your cars in.*

Strategy: If you have a two-car garage, you want to be able to get two cars in it comfortably when you sell your home, just to prove it can be done. You may wish to rent a small storage room temporarily for the items you will be moving to your next home.

9. *You are really getting into the spirit of your "clear out the clutter" project and are giving so much material to local charities that you begin to wonder if you should keep special records for income tax purposes.*

Strategy: At a minimum, you should write down each item and indicate the original cost to you and the condition and value on the date you donated it. There are special rules for high-value items. Check with the IRS or your accountant to make certain you get the most up-to-date information, because the ground rules and procedures change. What doesn't change is the requirement for accurate documentation.

10.   You decide to move your Hummel figurine collection to a more prominent spot in your living room to dress things up a little.

Strategy: It is unwise to leave anything of value on display when you are showing your home, particularly if it is of a fragile nature and it's expensive. The Hummels could be inadvertently broken or they could be stolen. I would advise you to carefully pack them away for another day.

6

·····▼·····

Selling the Homestead

You will have one very important decision to make early in your homeselling challenge: whether to sell it yourself or to employ a real estate broker to do it for you. Although the fundamental process is identical, and although you must be familiar with basic real estate matters in either instance, in one scenario you will be getting a great deal of help and guidance at each step. In the other instance, you will be handling most of the details yourself and making important decisions without the benefit of input from a real estate professional. There's a lot riding on your decision.

To List or Not To List

If you are planning to buy a home, it will generally be in your best interest to work with a real estate agent. There are exceptions, and even when you work with an agent you must be an active and informed participant, but that's a conclusion I've reached based upon my own experiences as both a consumer and as a REALTOR®. Although I generally recommend that homesellers also use an agent, I have to admit that the case for hiring a broker is not always quite as clear-cut.

Agency: Red-Hot Issue of the '90s

Before I outline the major advantages and disadvantages of listing with a broker, we need to pause and discuss the issue that is consuming and confounding state legislatures, real estate professionals and consumers alike—agency relationships in real estate transactions. This can be confusing the first time through, but please be patient and don't get discouraged. If you are informed (you soon will be), conduct yourself in a manner dictated by real world realities and choose your advisers carefully, you will be able to operate in a manner that will fully protect your own interests.

Agency: The Basics

Agency is a relationship created when one individual (the agent) receives the authority to act for another individual (the principal) in a business transaction. There is a large body of both statutory and common law that describes and regulates the relationship between principal and agent. There is also a rapidly growing number of laws at the state level that control the agency relationship between real estate licensees and the consumer.

Agency: The Real Estate Connection

When you sign a listing agreement with a real estate broker, that broker becomes your agent and is authorized to act for you to perform certain specified tasks in a well-defined area—marketing your home. In the role of agent, the broker has established a fiduciary relationship with the principal—you. Textbooks on law typically indicate that a fiduciary relationship means that the agent has the following responsibilities to the principal: confidentiality, obedience, accounting, loyalty and disclosure. In everyday language, it simply means that in any transaction, the agent puts the principal's interests (your interests) before anyone else's (most assuredly including the broker's).

For years the system worked as follows: your broker-agent put your listing on the Multiple Listing Service (MLS), thereby offering subagency to all other member real estate brokers (along with an offer to share the commission), which for practical purposes was all the brokers in your marketing area. As subagents those brokers also represented you and owed you the same fiduciary duties. Who represented the buyers? Legally, no one, although when real estate licensees worked with buyer prospects, their actions often gave the clear impression that they were agents of the buyer. That's because for all practical purposes they probably were representing the buyer by doing such things as suggesting negotiating strategies and passing on what was supposed to be confidential information about why the property was for sale.

When there is a problem in a real estate transaction, who is typically the disgruntled party? Statistically, homebuyers bring lawsuits much more often than homesellers. So when unhappy homebuyers went to an attorney and complained about the sorry condition of the home they just purchased, it was quite likely that the attorney, well versed in the laws of agency, would focus on that issue. Prove that there was an agency misrepresentation (the buyers were led to believe the broker working with them was their agent) and generally that was all that was needed to win the suit.

The resultant consumer unrest, fueled by many real estate brokers who saw an opportunity to step into a newly emerging market niche, led to the buyer-broker movement. In this arrangement, real estate brokers represent buyers and assume the same fiduciary responsibility that listing brokers have to sellers. The offer was hard for buyers to refuse because the agents typically expected to be paid the commission that the seller paid to the listing broker, in the same manner as was done under the subagency concept.

Agency: Follow the Money Trail

What are the practical implications for the homeowner who lists with a broker? First, that broker will be your agent and is supposed to be putting your interests first. Second, in many parts of the country, subagency is still the norm—all the other brokers with whom your broker cooperates will be representing you. Third, you are increasingly likely to encounter brokers who are representing buyers. In the overwhelming majority of cases, they expect to be paid from the transaction, which means the commission you pay.

To understand how this whole issue of agency relates to the actual homebuying and homeselling process, do what all astute investigators do: follow the money trail. Real estate brokers get paid when and if the transaction closes. That means they must satisfy everyone, and that's the force that motivates them. Even though you will be paying the commission, you will be getting the money to do that from the buyer.

Unless everyone stays happy until money and deed changes hands, there's no payday for any real estate professional involved. The attorneys, yes; the brokers, no.

The practical implications? First, if there is a buyer's broker involved in the transaction, do not tell that person anything you would not want the buyer to know. Second, be open and honest with your listing broker, but be cautious and do not reveal more than you need to. For example, let's say that you were to divulge to your agent your bottom-line price. Might not there be just the slightest temptation for the broker to pass along that information if it looked as though that were the only way to get a hot prospect to make an offer and realize a quick close? Essentially, your goals and your broker's are the same: sell your home for the highest price possible, because the more you receive for it, the more the broker makes. Further, if you hire a REALTOR® with advanced professional designations (we'll discuss that shortly), you will likely be working with an individual with extremely high personal and professional standards.

Working with a Broker: The Pros

Let's say you call several local real estate brokers and inform each that you are planning to sell your home and want to know if they would be interested in stopping by and giving you an idea of what it's worth and how they would market it if you gave them the listing.

First, expect an enthusiastic response from each and a determined effort to set a firm date and time for an appointment to come out and look at your home. Real estate brokers love listings because they are the inventory of their business. One cliché in the industry is that when you sell your last listing you've had your going-out-of-business sale. For the most common type of listing (called an exclusive right to sell) no matter who sells the house, the listing broker gets paid. That means that the moment they sign you up and inform other agents (with whom they promise to share the brokerage fee), they have hordes of enthusiastic compatriots beating the bushes for buyers.

We will assume that you schedule appointments with three brokers, based on your evaluation of your telephone conversations. Trust me when I say that you will hear some convincing arguments from some masters of persuasion: first, they'll tell you that you'll be much better off listing the home rather than trying to sell it yourself; second, the particular agent giving the presentation will argue that he or she is the person with whom you should sign on.

Real estate brokers honestly believe that you will be far better off working with them, because they are convinced that they are better equipped than you to sell your home in the shortest amount of time possible with the fewest problems. Further, when the smoke clears and the transaction is completed, they are convinced that you are likely to have more money in your pocket than if you sold it yourself. You, on the other hand, may feel that their objectivity is somewhat suspect in that in one scenario they stand to collect a tidy fee while in the other they will earn nothing. That's an understandable skepticism, so let's analyze the opposing arguments more closely. First, the advantages of working with a broker.

It's a Jungle Out There

An incredible amount of work goes into marketing a home properly and seeing the transaction through to a successful close when a ready, willing, and able buyer is found. The best way to demonstrate that is to list for you in outline form a checklist that a real estate agent might use in securing and servicing a listing. Most real estate companies will have a much more detailed standard checklist which their agents follow, which will incorporate such things as mandatory disclosure items. We will develop many of these ideas in more depth as we proceed, but this will give you a feel for the myriad of details that are involved. In the real world, a couple of agents may perform these tasks, because companies cooperate on sales in many transactions.

As you are going through this you may ask, "Do they really do all these things?" If your agent is on the ball (and I readily admit that not all of them are) they do all these things and more. You see, unless and until your transaction successfully closes, there is no payday for them. That's a very powerful motivator.

In researching this particular point I've relied heavily on training books written for real estate agents. Danielle Kennedy is one of the true superstars in the profession and is a prolific author and popular speaker. Here's the guidance she gives agents in her book, *How To List and Sell Real Estate in the '90s:* "So, sit yourself down, the morning after each sale, and think through everything that must be done to get that transaction closed, and your share of the fee safely tamped down in your bank account. Go over the purchase agreement's special provisions word-by-word; review the negotiations step-by-step; . . . Complete a special checklist for that closing as you do that. Then check your list regularly. Keep everything moving. You're the one who gets paid—or doesn't get paid—for doing all this." From listing to close, here are some of the things an agent would be doing. Don't be confused by the term *escrow*. It's not used in all states, but someone else will be performing the function.

• •

Screaming Eagle Realty Countdown to Payday: Listing/Sales Checklist

1. Make appointment with owner for listing presentation.

2. Secure listing packet from title company that will include official legal description, recorded easements and encumbrances and plat map of property showing property dimensions.

3. If property has recorded CC&Rs or restrictive covenants, get copies made to present to any potential purchaser prior to writing a formal offer.

4. Verify from local property taxing authority the assessed value of the home and the annual property taxes.

5. Determine whether property is in flood plain. If yes, brief seller on disclosure requirements and specialized insurance considerations.

6. Determine whether property is in geologically active area. If yes, discuss disclosure and insurance requirements.

7. Brief seller on the necessity of full disclosure of material facts and the specifics of any state-mandated specialized disclosure items and forms.

8. Prepare a competitive market analysis to determine suggested listing price. Get another opinion from at least one other agent.

9. Counsel seller on the function of title insurance and who customarily pays for various coverages.

10. Sign listing agreement with owner.

11. Prepare a preliminary "seller's net" sheet that shows how much the owner can expect at close after deducting expenses of sale, assuming a full-price offer.

12. Present owner with *How To Dress Your Home For Success* brochure and discuss specific methods of sprucing-up proerty.

13. Determine whether any boundary problems may exist or whether there are potential encroachments. If so, recommend a formal land survey be performed.

14. Inquire as to whether there are any unrecorded liens on the property or special property tax-deferral programs. If there are, discuss disclosure requirements.

15. Counsel owner on the benefits of purchasing a home warranty program for the buyer. Present brochure that describes home warranties.

16. Present owner with individualized marketing plan for the property.

17. Fill out notice to Multiple Listing and submit. Notify all other agents in central and branch offices immediately.

18. Compose advertising copy and submit to broker for approval.

19. Send "just listed" notes to all in immediate neighborhood.

20. Arrange for photo of property.

21. Process paperwork for home warranty.

22. Put up For Sale sign with warranty rider and agent name rider on it.

23. Prepare copy for property flyer and reproduce. Provide all agents in office a copy as well as each office in multiple listing.

24. Place box on property with flyer in it for drive-by prospects.

25. Obtain key from owner and put lockbox on property.

26. Contact mortgage company by letter to verify mortgage balance and whether it is assumable and under what conditions.

27. Brief owners on security concerns and safeguarding valuables during term of listing.

28. Schedule immediate tour of property by office agents and by agents from other offices on Multiple Listing on next official tour date.

29. Follow up on feedback from agents who toured home on pricing and suggestions for marketing.

30. Schedule an open house. Advertise in paper, notify neighbors, conduct open house. Follow up on each open-house attendee.

31. Coordinate and schedule individual showings for home.

32. Follow up with agent who conducts each showing to determine prospects' reaction to both the property and the price.

33. Present all offers to purchase to owner immediately after coordinating with broker.

34. Prior to presenting offer, insure that buyer has been properly and thoroughly qualified financially and that there are no problems.

35. Prepare a final "seller's net" sheet for owner when an offer has been accepted for a specific price, showing expenses of sale and how much will be received at close.

36. Review accepted offer in detail for contingencies and deadlines.

37. Prepare a checklist with each contingency listed, the person responsible for removing it, and the specific date by which it must be removed. Log each on individual calendar and review and follow up each day until all contingencies are removed and both buyer and seller have signed off on each.

38. Put "sale pending" sign on property.

39. Immediately turn in earnest money deposit to broker for deposit in clients' trust account.

40. If earnest money deposit is promissory note, follow up to insure it is redeemed as stipulated and then deposit immediately in clients' trust account.

41. Follow up to insure that purchaser applies for loan within time limit stipulated in offer to purchase.

42. Coordinate with lending institution to determine whether there are any potential problems with either the buyer or the property.

43. Find out from the lender when an appraisal might be expected.

44. Arrange for general property inspection to include asbestos assessment.

45. Arrange for radon inspection.

46. Arrange for pest and dry rot inspection if not included in general inspection.

47. Follow on all inspections by telephone immediately after they are conducted to determine if there are problems. Find out when the formal reports may be expected.

48. Insure that buyer has obtained required fire and hazard insurance policy and that a binder is available for escrow.

49. If the buyer is going to move into the property prior to close (counsel seller not to permit this) insure that proper rental agreement has been signed and insurance coverage is appropriate.

50. If repairs are needed to property, follow up to insure they are scheduled and completed satisfactorily.

51. Open escrow.

52. Review preliminary title report to see if there are any potential problems.

53. Check with closing officer every few days to see how the process is proceeding and whether there are any items with which you may assist.

54. Conduct final walk-through inspection with buyers. Resolve any problems.

55. Review formal closing documents at least 24 hours prior to close. Recommend to both buyer and seller that they do the same.

56. Remind buyer that a certified check will be required for amount due at close.

57. Attend closing.

58. Pick up lockbox, sign and send notes to neighbors introducing new residents.

59. Present closing gift to seller and give copy of critique form for them to fill out.

60. Deposit commission check in bank account!

• •

Buyers Are Sometimes Liars

If you have never dealt with the general public in a sales job, it will be difficult for you to appreciate how much of a challenge it really is to work with buyers. The major problem is that not all of them are completely honest with you 100 percent of the time. You will even occasionally run in to a few who you may have reason to suspect could be candidates for the FBI's top ten list. Then there is also a small but determined group whose major pastime in life seems to be looking at houses—looking, mind you, not buying.

Experienced and successful real estate agents, being magna cum laude graduates of the school of hard knocks, have learned to be good judges of character and to separate fact from fancy and hype from truth. That's why they are experienced and successful. Their livelihood depends upon it, as does the longevity of the broker who supervises the entire enterprise. There are also a number of institutional checks and balances built into the system designed to verify character, capability and intent.

Champagne Tastes—Beer Budgets

You already know that real estate agents perform a variety of important tasks in marketing a home and seeing the transaction through to a successful close. One of their most critical functions is to qualify potential buyers. That simply means that they find out early in the relationship how much of a loan the purchasers will qualify for when they submit their application. If the people who want to buy your home can't afford it, nothing else makes much difference.

People who attempt to sell their own homes quite often neglect to find out what potential purchasers can afford. They naively assume that if someone is looking at their house, they can afford to buy it. For many rookie real estate agents, it is one of the most difficult skills to master, because it does seem kind of tacky so early in a relationship to be asking prospects such personal questions as how much money they make, the size of their bank account, how many bills they have, and whether they have ever been bankrupt or returned a home back to a lender in lieu of foreclosure. It is, however, a survival technique agents simply must perfect very quickly. There are diplomatic ways to do it, but those questions have to get asked of new customers soon after "Please have a seat." There's very little point in driving people around town showing them the most expensive homes in the suburban hills when all they can afford is a modest bungalow in the flats.

I once spent two weeks showing expensive homes to a couple who convinced me with their big talk and fancy wardrobes that they could buy any house they wanted. I got giddy just contemplating what my share of the commission was going to be on a high six-figure sale. To be charitable, let's just say that their desires exceeded their financial capability—by a wide margin. They kept suggesting creative financing techniques unfamiliar outside of San Quentin, so no formal offers were ever written. All I wasted was my time and was saved further embarrassment by a grumpy broker who insisted that I do some discreet checking. If you, the homeowner, get conned, the consequences could be more dire, particularly if you have agreed to some form of owner financing.

Beating the Drums

One of the biggest advantages of listing your home with a broker is the market exposure that it will get. That's critical, because it makes little difference how great a bargain your home may be if no one knows about it. The most widely known marketing vehicle is the Multiple Listing Service (MLS). Although there are organizational differences, the basic function of what agents refer to simply as "multiple" is to get listed properties the widest possible market exposure. The service accomplishes that task well. Immediately upon listing your home, a small army of dedicated real estate professionals whose well-being depends in large part upon finding buyers for properties like yours hits the pavement running.

There are a variety of other promotional techniques that brokers use to display their wares. Newspaper display ads are commonplace, as are the more elaborate "Homes" magazines. In more and more localities you can now tune in to a real estate homes for sale show on television and even the information superhighway is getting into the act. To make certain that they go where the traffic is, brokers are now setting up displays, often manned by agents with computers and video screens, in airline terminals and shopping centers.

While it is true that some of these marketing vehicles are opening access to individuals selling their homes on their own, broker listings dominate the system.

The Art of the Deal

Although American consumers may not have a great reputation as hagglers in the marketplace, they do seem to be convinced that you never pay sticker price for a new car and you never make a full price offer on a home (unless it's new). They are so convinced that it is very difficult to persuade them that in some markets it is wise to offer **more** than full price for a home.

One of a broker's more delicate jobs is to convince both buyers and sellers that they are involved in a business transaction and that it is a good strategy to be as dispassionate as possible. For example, let's say a young couple has finally saved enough money for a down payment on a home and after extensive searching have found what they are convinced is their dream cottage. Having been told by their parents never to pay full price, they offer $5,000 less than asking price. The offer is rejected. They are crushed. No matter how much the broker reassures them that the rejection was of their offer, not of them, they retreat into a shell. And hell hath no fury like homeowners who get what we in the business call low ball offers on their beloved homesteads.

Real estate agents who have been involved in transactions such as these come to regard themselves as educators and counselors as much as salespeople. Those who are successful in the profession become very good at fulfilling these roles. From early in any relationship, they provide needed guidance, convincing the participants that although home-buying and homeselling are certainly emotional experiences, goals will more likely be achieved if the participants can take a step back and become as dispassionate as is reasonably possible.

Working with a Broker: The Cons

If real estate agents do all of these wonderful things, what on earth would motivate anyone to try to sell their home themselves? Simple. Money. Let's say your home's market value is $150,000. If you pay a 6 percent commission (brokerage fee) that's 9,000 big ones. That's enough to make anyone do some serious thinking about the decision. Then there's also the concern that you may hire a broker to sell your home and end up getting a lemon of a real estate agent. I will have some suggestions for you that help you avoid that nightmare, so you can make your decision based upon other factors.

Meet the Fizzbos

Those who attempt to sell their homes themselves are affectionately known in the business as FSBOs (for sale by owner, pronounced "Fizzbo"). For the Red Flag Checklist in this chapter, I've composed a list of questions designed to help you determine whether you want to go it on your own. If that turns out to be your decision, there is an entire chapter designed to help you successfully achieve your goals. But please, Fizzbo or not, read the entire book! There's vital information you will need throughout.

Red Flag Checklist
Fizzbo Yes? Fizzbo No?

1.   Are you prepared to do the research needed to determine the fair market value of your home?

There's plenty of no-cost, willing help available and I'll describe how to plug into that resource, but it will take time and effort, as opposed to what some broker's accuse Fizzbos of doing: making a WAG (wild astrological guess).

2.   Are you willing to put your home on the market at or near fair market value?

This is critical whether you sell your home yourself or list it with a broker, but I've seen so many Fizzbos get so hopelessly wrapped around the axle on this particular point that it deserves your special attention. There's an entire chapter on this topic, so stay tuned.

3.   Do you have the time to do the job right?

Spend a few minutes going back over the listing checklist earlier in the chapter. I hope you are impressed with the amount of work that's required, and it's just a bare-bones overview. Although it's true that you would not have to do some of those things if you handled the job yourself, most of them need to be done, and some of them require a great deal of time. For example, talking to prospective purchasers and showing your home not only takes time but can come at extremely inconvenient hours.

4.   Do you have the knowledge to do the job right?

There is a lot to know, and your lack of knowledge could cost you big bucks or even get you embroiled in a nasty lawsuit. At a minimum, you must educate yourself well enough on the whole procedure to know when you are on dangerous ground and need to call up the reserves, which leads to my next question:

5.   *Are you willing to hire a lawyer?*

Some people would rather eat dirt than spend a few hundred dollars for the services of an attorney. It may be the fact that I live in a comparatively small town and all the lawyers have to pretty much behave themselves, but I firmly believe that it is foolhardy not to obtain competent legal advice on matters as important as buying or selling a home. I even counsel hiring an attorney when you list your home with a broker. If you are soloing, it is even more critical. Here's a phrase I suggest you use frequently when talking to real estate agents and/or prospective purchasers: "That sounds pretty good, but of course I'll have to run it by my attorney before I commit myself." You would be amazed at what impact that has on a conversation. Of course, for maximum results you have to have an attorney to run it by.

6.   *Are you emotionally equipped to handle negotiations with a purchaser?*

Are you tough enough to be firm, yet realistic enough to be reasonable? Do discussions over such things as price and terms produce acid in your stomach or get your adrenalin flowing?

7.   *Can you detach yourself emotionally and treat the entire enterprise as a business transaction?*

If someone makes an insultingly low offer on your home, can you retain your composure and coolly write up a counteroffer?

8.   *How hot is the market?*

A hot market is called a seller's market. That typically happens when the nation's economy is on an even keel and mortgage interest rates are low. Local circumstances, such as the relocation of a large business that employs thousands of highly paid workers, will have an obvious impact on the housing market. The end result is more buyers than sellers and homes going near, at or above their asking price. In some really hot markets, about all you would have to do is stick a sign in the front yard and sort out the offers. Naturally, you would still run everything by your attorney.

9.   How desirable is your home?

It's going to be hard to be objective on this one, but if you do in fact have a desirable (or unique) piece of property, then the job of selling it will be much easier. Even in a buyer's market (lots of homes for sale, high interest rates and few qualified buyers) a highly sought after home will sell quickly and for a good price.

10.   How motivated are you to sell?

If you must be on the new job in Fargo in 90 days and you have to sell your home to get enough money to buy a new one, you will be highly motivated and under severe time constraints. Most people in that circumstance will find the best real estate broker they can, price their homes at or slightly under market, and be very reasonable in negotiations. If, on the other hand, it makes no particular difference to you how quickly your home sells (or for that matter, whether or not it sells), then you may be more inclined to give it a go on your own.

• •

Decisions, Decisions, Decisions

Not only do you have a lot of important decisions to make, it helps to get the sequence right. Many people decide first whether to list their home or sell it themselves, and then they decide what they are going to ask for it. There's really nothing wrong with that, but I'm going to suggest that a better course of action would be for you to first determine your asking price and **then** make a final judgment on whether to hire a broker. I'll explain my rationale for that recommendation in detail in the next chapter on pricing, but at this point let me simply say that how much your home is worth on the open market has absolutely nothing to do with whether you list it or not. Now that I have your attention, please read on.

7

·····▼·····

Pricing Your Palace

Whether you join the ranks of the Fizzbos or you employ a real estate broker to market your property for you, you've got a critical decision to make early in the game: how much are you going to ask for your home?

There is so much fuzzy-headed thinking on this subject, and people become so emotionally involved, that no matter how well informed you believe you are, I need to ask you to defer any final decisions until you've considered all of the evidence. One of the nice things about writing a book is that when I give you advice you may not want to hear, I don't have to see your face turn red in indignation. If I were sitting in your living room giving a listing presentation, my goal would be to have you hire me. The last thing I would want to do would be to alienate you by suggesting that you may be hallucinating when you tell me your asking price. On the other hand, the news could be much better than you expected, so sit back and relax.

What's It Really Worth?

Professional, licensed real property appraisers are in the business of making informed judgments on the value of specific pieces of real estate. When you apply for a home loan, for example, the whole process stops until the lending institution hires (and you pay for) an appraiser to evaluate the property to determine if it is worth what they plan to loan on it. Appraisers have a technical term, *market value*. That's what those grim-faced, no-nonsense loan officers at the bank want to know, for if the worst happens and they have to foreclose on the property, they want to be assured that they will likely get back what they have loaned on it.

Market Value: Theory

The *Arnold Encyclopedia of Real Estate* defines market value as "the most probable price expressed in terms of money that a property would bring if exposed for sale in the open market in an arm's length transaction between a willing seller and a willing buyer, both of whom are knowledgeable concerning all the uses to which it is adapted and for which it is capable of being used." Although the word *guess* is seldom used by appraisers, that's really what they do, because no one actually knows what a property will sell for until it's put on the market. When that happens, the market itself determines market price.

Appraisers would prefer the term *informed opinion*. To be fair, they do employ some rigorous procedures to arrive at their conclusions. For example, when they assign a market value to a property, they do so using the following assumptions, which were developed by a professional organization, the Appraisal Institute, and described in their reference book, *The Dictionary of Real Estate Appraisal.*

1. The sale is completed as of a specific date.

2. An open and competitive market exists.

3. The buyer and seller are each acting prudently and knowledgeably.

4. The price is not affected by undue stimulus.

5. The buyer and seller are typically motivated.

6. Both parties are acting in what they consider their best interests.

7. Marketing efforts are adequate and a reasonable time is allowed for exposure in the open market.

8. Payment is made in cash in U.S. dollars or another comparable financial arrangement.

9. The price represents the normal consideration for the property sold, unaffected by special or creative financing or sales concessions granted by anyone associated with the sale.

Market Value: Practice

As a homeseller, you want to know the market value of your home—what it's likely to sell for when you expose it to the open market, taking into account all the theoretical niceties and assuming a normal, arms-length transaction.

Let's say you follow the suggestions given later in this chapter and you decide that your home has a market value of $125,000. Your next step is to decide on your asking price. Typically, homeowners ask more for their homes than they expect to get to permit room for negotiation. There are those who counsel against that, but that's the reality of it. Even in hot seller's markets, the average price paid for homes is typically slightly less than asking price. In buyer's markets, it can be substantially less. So we will say you put your property on the market for $130,000 and accept an offer of $127,500. That means market value $125,000; asking price $130,000; market price $127,500.

Help Wanted

So how much should *I* ask for *my* house? At this point, you need to call in help. You could hire an appraiser, but that would cost you several hundred dollars and you can get the same basic service free. I suggest you call at least three local real estate brokers and tell them you are planning to sell your home and want their input on pricing and marketing before you make your final decision on who you are going to list it with or whether to sell it yourself.

Now even if you have firmly and absolutely decided that you are absolutely not going to list your home with any real estate agent, don't skip the following information. You should still invite at least three of them to your house to give you their listing presentations.

Is that approach really fair to the real estate agents? Absolutely. Getting good listings is critical to survival, and a confident, successful agent only wants a time at bat. Let's say you call me and I give you my listing presentation. What are the possible outcomes for me? One, you could be so dazzled by my consummate professionalism and charm that you immediately change you attitude toward real estate agents and list your home with me. Two, you could decide to sell it yourself and then get so sick of the whole mess that you call me to come quickly to your rescue. Three, you could list it yourself and successfully sell it, based largely on the expert guidance I provided you. Hopefully, you would then so grateful that you would recommend me to all your friends and acquaintances, and when you had a real estate need in the future you might very well think of me. Of course, I would much prefer options one or two, but three is perfectly acceptable. If the unthinkable happens and you list your home with a competing agent after hearing my presentation, then I just have to figure out what I did wrong or someone else did better and learn from my experience. This is a competitive business, so don't worry about hurting anyone's feelings.

Who Are You Going To Call?

Your first chore is to decide which three brokerage firms in your area are the most active and most successful. You can get a good feel for that by reading, listening to and watching the real estate ads in the local media and by talking to people. It will also help to drive around town and observe the number of For Sale signs in various neighborhoods, particularly yours and those similar to yours. After narrowing the field, swing by the various offices to take a look. Do they reflect a prosperous, businesslike atmosphere or do you have to go up three flights of stairs, knock twice and say "Joe sent me"?

If the real estate agents where you live are really on the ball, one or several of them will be "farming" your neighborhood. That means they are doing everything they can to let you know they are in business and that they want yours. If they listed a home down the street from you, they will let you know, and they will certainly inform you when they sell it.

After you've decided which brokerage firms to contact, it is time to call them and ask to have an agent come by for a listing presentation. It is very important that you specify that the agent they send meet certain very specific criteria.

I can best illustrate my recommendations on this point by relating a personal experience of my own. Several years ago, when I was actively selling real estate in Oregon, I had to go to California to settle my mother's estate. The major item of business was to sell her modest little home. I knew no one in the business where she lived, so I followed the advice I just gave you. I knew I didn't have time to sell the home myself, so I had already decided to list it. When I called each broker I said I wanted to hear from an agent who:

1. Was a REALTOR®. You can actually tell this by reviewing the ads of the brokerage firm itself, since if they display the REALTOR® sign all of the agents in the office are probably going to be REALTORS®, but you should still verify. You want a REALTOR® because they have agreed to abide by a code of ethics and are expected to display high standards of conduct. Obviously not all of them do, but you'll improve your chances.

2. Worked full time in the real estate profession.

3. Specialized in residential sales.

4. Had several active listings and several successfully closed listings in the immediate past.

5. Possessed the Graduate REALTOR® Institute (GRI) or the Certified Residential Specialist (CRS) professional designations. These are REALTOR® designations. To get the GRI you must successfully complete a series of three weeklong courses. To get the CRS you must take additional coursework beyond the GRI and demonstrate competence by successfully completing a specified number of residential transactions. I am a great believer in professional education, no matter what the profession. Those who pursue it are typically people who take their work seriously and are not afraid to spend the time, effort and money to increase their knowledge—and their income. Don't compromise on this point. Insist on a GRI or CRS as a minimum to get in your door.

I interviewed three agents. Each was very professional. The woman I selected had the CRS. Let me tell you, she was good. I listed the home with her and we sold it in less than two weeks at full price but with an agreement to pay a couple of the buyers' loan points. There were no hassles and no misunderstandings. The buyers were also satisfied because they got a nice home at a fair price.

Preparing for the Pitch

When you get the listing presentation, you will receive a detailed analysis of pricing. That's great, because at this point that's the main reason you are having the agents over. You will also get a personal sales job, because the agent's goal is to have you list on the spot. Some

agents can be very convincing. They can also be persistent and sometimes even a little pushy, so you must be pleasant but firm. At this
point you just want to hear from all parties before making any decisions on price or with whom you will list or whether you will sell on
your own.

Most agents will give you their opinion of the likely price range in
which your home falls, the market value (what it's really worth) and
the suggested asking price. Some will give you everything but the actual suggested asking price but will furnish information in such detail
that it is clear what they think it should be.

Sizing Up the Competition

The formal name for the process real estate agents use in arriving at
this information is called the competitive market analysis (CMA). Real
estate appraisers use basically the same technique to value most residential properties; they call it the sales comparison approach. It is
based on a simple concept despite its fancy name: substitution. That
means that the maximum value of any property tends to be set by the
cost of purchasing an equally desirable and valuable substitute property. In other words, faced with a decision, why would someone buy
your home for $130,000 when several equally desirable properties are
available at $125,000?

Here's an example of how it works. When we bought our new home
in Walnut Creek, California, in 1966, we paid $30,000 for it. It was in a
large subdivision where all the homes were constructed by the same
builder. There were four basic models, available with slight variations
if you bought the home before it was completed and paid for the
changes. Ours was the least expensive—we'll call it the Brooktree.
Within a few blocks in any direction there were at least four or five
other Brooktrees constructed by the same builder at approximately the
same time. During the four years we lived there, several came on the
market and sold: it was an active market.

When we interviewed real estate agents, each presented us with a
CMA. On that CMA was indicated: (1) homes like ours (remember,
there were several others exactly like ours within the immediate area)
that had sold recently and the price that was paid for each; (2) homes
like ours that were currently on the market (the competition) and the
asking price of each; and (3) homes like ours that had been on the

market but did not sell during the listing period. As I recall, the market was so good then that there were none in this category.

In addition, the agents presented us with a recommended pricing strategy. The format of each CMA varied somewhat, as did the personal styles of the agents, but the basic guidance we got included the price range in which our house was likely to sell, the actual price for which it was likely to sell (the agent's estimate of market value), and the suggested asking price, which in each case was higher than the anticipated sales price. Because we seemed a bit more impressed with some of the improvements we had made than the agents seemed to be, and because I had a great assumable GI loan, we opted for the highest figure in the suggested range and listed it and sold it for that amount.

I recognize that this process sounds extremely complex, and at one time it was. However, with the advent of computer technology a competent real estate agent can complete a CMA for you in a short time. As a matter of fact, some in the appraisal industry are beginning to express concern that their profession may be in jeopardy. Why pay an appraiser several hundred dollars for a job that a computer can help you do almost instantaneously?

The technology is even becoming available to consumers, so if you are computer literate, check with others with similar interests and see if the product is accessible.

Bullet-Biting Time

Armed with all of your individual research and based on the input you've received during the listing presentations, you now must decide on a specific asking price for your home. You are clear on which factors you should consider, but how about those that are irrelevant? Take a deep breath, relax, and keep an open mind as I pursue this point, because some (but not all) of the guidance is typically not what homeowners want to hear.

Say What?

The following have absolutely no bearing on how much your home is worth:

1. How much you paid for it. In the best of all possible worlds your home will appreciate in value while you own it and you will sell it for a nice profit. It is not, however, an inalienable right. Your home is worth what a buyer will pay for it now. What you paid for it is irrelevant to them.

    I should point out that this process sometimes works in reverse, and those who sell their own homes without even getting input from real estate professionals are particularly likely to make a pricing mistake. Some people have difficulty believing that their houses have appreciated as much as they may have. The fact that you bought it for $50,000 fifteen years ago and it's worth $150,000 now (and you couldn't afford to buy it now) may seem hard to believe, but it could well be true. Find out!

2. Whether you list it with a real estate broker or not. The fact that you may pay 5, 6 or 7 percent commission is an irrelevant consideration in pricing your home and is not justification for deciding upon a fair price and then tacking on the commission to arrive at your asking price. All buyers will see is your asking price, and it had better be competitive or they'll mosey on down the street.

3. How much you have to get out of it to pay off your mortgage and other expenses of the sale and have enough left over to make a down payment on another home. Hopefully, you will have more than enough to cover all expenses and end with a tidy surplus. But put yourself in a buyer's shoes. Would you care what the sellers did with the money you paid for their house?

4. How much you paid for improvements to the house. The fact that you've spent $50,000 on a major remodeling job has unquestionably added value to your home. It is quite unlikely, however, that it added dollar-for-dollar value. Buyers will consider your home as a total package. Decisions on home improvements should be based primarily upon life-style choices and only secondarily on how much value they may add to the home. Some improvements actually detract from the value of a home in the eyes of certain buyers. Some people, for example, would never buy a home with a swimming pool.

5. How much your Cousin Murray in Topeka got for his dinky home when he sold it. Because you live in San Antonio, it doesn't make

much difference what your cousin got for his place in Topeka. Besides, you know how Murray tends to exaggerate.

Finally! Pick a Number

If everything has gone according to plan, you are now ready to make an informed decision about how much to ask for your home. You may not yet have decided whether to list it, but you're sure of your answer when someone asks you how much you want for it. Just to put further pressure on you to make the right call, consider these final comments.

Pick the Right Number

You will have a good feel for the anticipated price range of your home. Where you place it in that range will depend primarily on how motivated you are to sell. The higher you place it in that range, the more probable it is that you will have difficulty selling it. Let me explain how the typical MLS operates and how real estate agents work with buyers to illustrate it. Although the discussion relates mainly to listing your home with a broker, the same general principles apply if you are selling it yourself. People shopping the Fizzbo market become very good judges of value.

Properties are grouped in the MLS by classification (residential, rural, investment, etc.) and by price range within each category, starting with the lowest priced and ending with the highest. Agents first qualify buyers and then show them homes within a general price range. For example, let's say I'm working with the Smedleys and together we've decided that they can qualify for and want to look at homes between $185,000 and $200,000. I check out all the possibilities in MLS in that range. Each day I check for new listings to see if there are any recent additions. I preview the possibilities and show the Smedleys the homes that best meet their stated needs and desires. I only show them homes between $185,000 and $200,000, although if something really promising came on the market for $182,500 I would obviously ask them if they wanted to take a peek. I would not, however, be likely to show them something that sounded like what they wanted but had a $205,000 price tag.

Let's assume that the best estimate of the market value of your home is somewhere between $190,000 and $200,000. Because you are convinced that it is worth at least $205,000, you list it for $209,000 and decide you would accept $205,000. The Smedleys and other buyers in that price range will never see it. Those who will see it are in the next higher group, and they will judge your home in comparison to those in that group. If the original inputs on pricing you got were correct, it's likely not to fare too well in that competition. None of the best potential buyers for your home may ever see it.

"I can always lower my price if it doesn't sell," you may say. That's true, but the most action you are going to get on home showings is going to be immediately after you first list it. That's because that's when many agents who are working with potential buyers are going to be most interested. If you're selling it yourself, the situation is much the same. People who notice your new ad in the paper or see your new sign in the front yard are typically the most motivated to take a look then. If it stays on the market unsold for a period of time, it becomes shopworn, and people begin to conclude there must be something wrong with it or it would have sold.

The Price Is Right

An old-time broker I know says about pricing homes, "Properly priced is practically sold." Of course, home valuation is an art, not a science, so your opinion may be just as good as anyone else's, and it is, after all, your property and your decision to make. I hope you will agree that you now have the unbiased information you need to make the best decision possible for your individual situation.

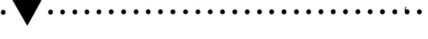

Red Flag Checklist and Survival Strategies

   1.   *You have decided to list your home and have scheduled interviews with three agents. Although your objective in having them over was to get input on pricing, the first one is so impressive that you decide to list with her on the spot and cancel the other two appointments.*

Strategy: Don't be so hasty. You may be even more impressed with numbers two and three. Remember your objective: to get pricing input.

2.   You have gotten glowing reports on a real estate agent from several sources you respect, including satisfied former customers of the agent, your attorney and some contacts at the title company. However, he works part time, dresses like the scarecrow from the Wizard of Oz, and is not a REALTOR®.

Strategy: You may have encountered what could be that rare exception to the rule. In any business, results count, as long as they are achieved honestly and efficiently. I would certainly check additional sources, but if they all verify what you've already been told, have the scarecrow over to give you a listing presentation.

3.   The first of the three agents you have scheduled turns out to be very aggressive and is pressing for an on-the-spot decision. He tells you he will be glad to call the other two agents you have scheduled and let them know you've listed with him.

Strategy: Aggressive is a good trait in real estate agents. You want that in someone who is trying to sell your home. Obnoxious, on the other hand, is a bad trait. You have to make the judgment, but I would still strongly counsel you to hear all three agents and get pricing information from each.

4.   After you hear one agent's listing presentation, you thank him and tell him you will think it over and get back to him with your decision. He doesn't take it well.

Strategy: "We'll think it over and get back to you" is like a dagger in the heart to many agents. They know that once they leave without the name on the dotted line, the probability of getting the listing decreases dramatically. Try to cushion the blow by letting everyone know up front that you are now just gathering information and that you will be deciding later.

5.   Two of the three agents you interview recommend a specific asking price for your home. The third gives you all the same basic information but keeps telling you that deciding on an asking price is your decision to make.

Strategy: Most agents will make a definite price recommendation, but there are those who don't want to incur your wrath if they do and things turn out badly. It is, in fact, your decision, and the basic information you get from each should be similar, so I wouldn't get too worked up over this one.

6.   *When you look at the business card of an agent who is scheduled for a listing presentation it does not include the designation GRI or CRS, although you specifically asked for an agent with one of those designations. When questioned, the agent says that she is "practically finished" with all the GRI requirements.*

Strategy: For me, that would end the interview. I like to work with people who know the difference between practically finished and finished.

7.   *Two of the three agents you interview give you a probable price range for your home between $175,000 and $180,000. The third says he thinks it's worth at least $195,000.*

Strategy: You've heard of lowball bids? I guess we could call this a highball bid. While it could be an honest difference of opinion, it may also be an attempt to get you so excited by the big numbers that you list with that agent. I would do some further investigation.

8.   *When giving her listing presentation one agent completely befuddles you with a discussion of the various types of deeds that you might give to a buyer of your home.*

Strategy: You should be aware that one technique used to convince homeowners to list with a broker is to make the whole thing sound so hopelessly complex that they break down and sign up on the spot. Figuring out which deed to give a buyer is not rocket science and your attorney is going to handle that for you anyhow.

9.   *An agent who is inspecting your house prior to his listing presentation points out that your hot water heater connection is corroded and looks as though it may emulate Old Faithful any moment.*

Strategy: Call the plumber to take a look. For those homeowners who may be intimidated by such things as corroded pipes and various objects such as furnaces and electrical fuse boxes, some agents try to prime the listing pump by pointing out dubious problems, thereby shaking the homeowner's confidence in handling their own affairs.

10. After interviewing agents to get market price input, you decided to list your home with a broker. You tell each of the three REALTORS® you interview that you will let them know your choice of agents in seven days. During that period, one of the agents contacts you to ask if she can provide any further information to help you make your decision. The other two do not call you.

Strategy: I personally would give the agent who called back a plus. You want a go-getter working for you—aggressive but not pushy. Let's say you listed your home and a prospect looked at it with your agent and told her, "I'll think it over." Would you want your agent to follow up?

8

· · · · · ▼ · · · · ·

Home Financing and the Golden Rule

The golden rule of home financing is simply this: those who have the gold make the rules. So, unless a buyer has the cash and is willing to part with it (rare), or has a rich aunt willing to advance the money (very rare), there's really no practical alternative to dealing with mortgage lenders. Fortunately, it's a competitive marketplace, and lending institutions stay in business by making loans. Or rather, they stay in business by making loans that people pay back. That's where the rules come in.

Who Needs This?

It's apparent why buyers need to know all about mortgages, but why should a seller be concerned? There's the obvious, of course. You are all in the pot together. No money for a loan, no money for the home. In addition, everything in a real estate transaction is negotiable. For example, there is no law that says the buyer has to pay for all of the costs associated with a getting a loan. As a result, you may be afforded the privilege of paying for some of them. What's more, depending upon the rest of the terms (full-price offer, for instance), you may agree.

Beyond these things, however, here are some other compelling reasons for learning as much as you can about mortgage lending. We'll cover them by category.

Fizzbos

Qualifying for the amount of the loan needed to buy your home will be a sink-or-swim issue with a very large number of your prospective purchasers, and it's remarkable how little some buyers know about the whole process. We'll get into more detail in the Fizzboing chapter, but if you are selling on your own and your attitude toward a buyer is "Don't ask me any questions about financing—that's up to you." you will be a lot less competitive than your neighbors down the street who have their home on the market and have done the homework required to talk intelligently and reassuringly to prospects.

Even more importantly, as a Fizzbo you will have to be able to act as your own initial screener and know how to qualify buyers, because you will not have a real estate agent to do that for you. That means you need to be aware of at least the basic fundamentals of financing and credit evaluation. It makes absolutely no difference how much that nice young couple likes your home or how impressed you are with them: if they don't have the needed up-front cash, the credit worthiness and the qualifying income, you're headed down a time-consuming and nerve-racking dead end. Unless, of course, you're willing to lower your price sufficiently for them to qualify, a course of action not typically recommended if you have any other options.

Homeowners Who Have Listed

As we will see in Chapter 9, a broker who has listed your home has one overriding goal: to produce a ready, willing and able buyer. The "ready and willing" part of the equation generally means that the buyer agrees with the offering terms and is willing to enter into a contract. "Able" is the critical discriminator. You would have no difficulty at all producing all sorts of anxious buyers if you didn't insist that they also have the financial capability. Because agents only get paid when transactions close, they get very good at judging buyer capability early in the game.

If you've got an agent doing this service for you, why numb your brain trying to understand even the elementary terms involved in financing? I will say this: if you've selected a broker who is a true professional and who is putting your interests ahead of everyone else's, then you can pretty much sit back and relax and be assured that everything will be taken care of pretty well. On the other hand, even if that is the case, wouldn't you feel a little better if you could at least enter intelligently into the conversations that relate to some important decisions you are going to have to make?

Owner Financing

In some instances, owners may act as their own bankers. The purest example would be an individual who owns a home free and clear and wants to handle everything, including receiving the monthly payments. It's also a fairly common practice for owners to take back a second mortgage. We'll develop these concepts in greater detail later in this chapter, but a common element is the need for sellers to be well informed to protect their interests.

Your Next Home

Most homesellers become homebuyers at some point in the future. Many do so almost immediately. If you will be buying again, it will be time well spent to get up to speed on the basics of mortgage lending.

Your Reading Assignment

Each spring I teach a course in real estate finance at the local community college. I'll be honest with you—it's not my favorite subject. I've always been more of a word person than a number person, so it's a real challenge to become informed and stay a couple of steps ahead of my students. One technique I use is to call in mortgage brokers and bankers to brief us all on current affairs. Another is to spend a lot of time with basic reference books. There are a number of good ones on the market, but the most informative one I've found for consumers is a book called *All About Mortgages,* by Julie Garton-Good (see bibliography). Garton-Good is a former real estate broker turned real estate educator and author. The book is in a question-and-answer format, and if there's a question you have that's not answered, I would be surprised. You will still need to keep up with more recent developments in the field, but this is an excellent primer.

Your Mortgage Menu

Hardly a month goes by without some new mortgage loan program appearing on the scene. Often these ventures have catchy names, but here are a buyer's basic choices.

Fixed Rate, Fixed Term, Fully Amortized

For many years this was the only option available to borrowers. Fixed rate means that if you start with a 10 percent loan, you end with a 10 percent loan. It also means that your monthly payment throughout the loan will be exactly the same. Fixed term means that you know from the start how long it will take to pay the loan off. Thirty years (360 monthly payments) is the most common, but 25-, 20- and 15-year terms are possible. Generally, the borrower gets a slight rate break on the shorter terms. Fully amortized means that when you make that last payment, your balance is zero. You own the home free and clear—unless, of course, you encumbered it with other loans in the meantime.

As a seller, you need to understand that this option is still preferred by most homebuyers. It's easy to understand and it offers the reassurance that you can budget for a monthly mortgage payment that will never change. To be more accurate, the monthly amount you pay for principal and interest (the "PI" of PITI) will never change. Property taxes and insurance (the "TI") can and frequently do. When you are investigating mortgage possibilities, use the rate lenders are charging for a fixed-rate, fixed-term, fully amortized loan as your benchmark. These rates are ordinarily slightly higher than other options, but they remain the top consumer preference. Always know those rates when you are talking to buyers and share the information with them.

Adjustable Rate Mortgages (ARMs)

If lenders could offer only one loan and stay in business, it would likely be some version of the ARM. The reason? The mortgage rate adjusts up and down based on an index, thereby providing the lending institutions protection against wild increases in interest rates. One of the major problems lenders had in the 1980s was that they had a lot of long-term, low-interest, fixed-rate mortgages on their hands. When interest rates shot out of sight and they had to start paying depositors more than they were realizing from their real estate loans, an obvious problem developed.

ARMs have a definite appeal to some buyers, mainly those who are on the borderline of being able to qualify. ARMs will carry a lower interest rate than a fixed-term loan, perhaps several percentage points lower. Because the buyers will be evaluated using the lower interest rate, their monthly payments will be considerably less, which could well mean the difference between being able to buy a home and not being able to do so. If you're working with young buyers just getting started on the salary scale, ARMs tend to be a frequent choice.

ARMs also appeal to buyers who plan to be in their homes for a comparatively short period of time. Most ARMs have limits on how much they may increase in one year and over the life of the loan. If an individual can get an ARM at a bargain rate and plans to sell before the worst-case scenario could result (that rate equaling the original cost of a fixed-rate loan) it makes good sense to go with an ARM.

Side Dishes

Keep in mind that the features of standard fixed-rate loans and of ARMs can be combined into one loan. For example, there is an arrangement called the convertible ARM that starts as an adjustable but at a predetermined point may be converted to a fixed rate.

There are a few other possibilities. Combined, they account for a tiny percentage of all mortgages in the United States. Here are a few of the more prominent ones.

Graduated Payment Mortgages (GPMs).   The borrower pays a lower monthly payment during the early years of the loan, which again means that they are more likely to qualify. The payments increase at some later point to make up for the lower initial payments. Negative amortization occurs during the early years because the payments do not cover the principal and interest due.

Shared Equity Mortgages (SEMs).   These loans are structured so that you have one party who is a non-owner-occupant investor and one who is an owner-occupant. These arrangements work well when one party has some money to invest for the down payment and the other party has the monthly income to qualify for a mortgage but no up-front cash. Depending on how they are structured, each party could own 50 percent of the property. Originally, SEMs were limited mainly to parents (the investors with the cash for the down payment) and children (the owner-occupants with no cash but a decent monthly income). In recent years, however, general investors have become more involved.

If you have anyone interested in your home who mentions a SEM, have them run, not walk, to the nearest attorney. Make certain he or she doesn't give you a blank stare when you mention the procedure. SEMs are complicated arrangements, and most people know just enough about them to be dangerous. You don't want to have your house tied up while all the details get sorted out. If they've got their act together up front, fine.

Shared Appreciation Mortgages (SAMs).   These loans sounded better in theory than they turned out to be in practice. Lenders would offer a discount mortgage rate in return for a share of the appreciation of the property when it sold. There were a couple of glitches. First, if there were no appreciation, there would be nothing to share. Second, the property either had to be sold or refinanced for the lender to realize any money. There may be some situations where this type of loan would work well, but both parties would need to be attentive to the provisions of the agreement.

FHA and VA

You will often hear the term "conventional loan" used. These are mortgage loans that are neither insured nor guaranteed by an agency of the federal government. The majority of the loans made each year in the United States are conventional loans. So which federal agencies are involved in mortgage lending and what do they do?

The Federal Housing Administration (FHA) insures loans and the Department of Veterans Affairs (VA) guarantees them. Mortgage lenders are protected to a certain extent against losses caused by default, which encourages them to make loans. People often think that FHA and VA offer only one type of plain vanilla loan—take it or leave it. Actually, they offer a wide selection of loans including the fixed-rate, fully amortized loan (which FHA pioneered) and many of the more exotic species. FHA, in particular, has been innovative. For example, they've got five different varieties of GPMs.

Federal Housing Administration

The FHA is a federal agency that has existed since the Great Depression. It was originally a part of what was called the National Housing Act and was designed to rescue a building industry that had collapsed during the depression.

The FHA's original goals were (1) to provide a method of home financing that was accessible and affordable to the American consumer, that was acceptable to the lending industry, and that could be sustained; (2) to stabilize the national mortgage market; and (3) to encourage improvement and standardization of housing construction regulations.

The FHA has done, and continues to do, an outstanding job in each of these areas. It has also typically required smaller down payments from borrowers and has permitted somewhat relaxed qualification standards. As a result, there have been years where FHA loans have comprised as much as 30 percent of all mortgage loans made in the United States.

Veterans Administration

The GI loan program was a product of the World War II era and was designed to assist returning veterans in buying affordable housing. It did so by guaranteeing a portion of any loan a lending institution made to a qualified GI. Because no down payment was a distinguishing characteristic of the loan, few lenders would have cared to participate without Uncle Sam's assurance that if they suffered a loss on the loan the government would stand behind a portion of it.

FHA and VA: The Rest of the Story

No one disputes that FHA and VA have been an incredibly positive influence on the country's housing market. I was able to buy my first home thanks to a no-money-down GI loan, and I financed a small rental property with an FHA loan (when they were making loans on investment properties). The programs are not, however, without their critics.

For years interest rates on their loans were regulated by the FHA and VA. That meant when you called a lender, you asked for the FHA rate, the VA rate, and the conventional rate. Because FHA and VA rates were typically lower than conventional rates, lending institutions added points to the cost of getting a loan. A point is 1 percent of the loan amount and is added to reflect what lenders call the true cost of the money. In many instances, lenders were prohibited by law from charging those points to buyers, which left the seller to pay them.

In addition, both programs featured what many thought were mind-boggling and needless rules and regulations. For these reasons, many homeowners who put their homes on the market would indicate on their listing or in their FSBO ad: "No FHA or VA." Some lending institutions have been known to refuse to handle FHA or VA loans simply because they don't wish to get involved with the bureaucracy and feel there's ample business in the conventional market.

As both programs have evolved, they have become more and more like conventional loans. In addition to limits on the size of the loans, the most distinguishing feature continues to be the higher loan-to-value ratios permitted—in other words, lower down payments. That means when you put your home on the market you will increase the pool of potential buyers considerably by agreeing to FHA or VA financing. Will it be worth the added hassle? For me, it would depend upon how marketable my house was. If I thought I could sell it with conventional financing with no problem, that would probably be my first choice.

Loan Assumptions: Attention Please!

If you've found your attention wandering and your eyeballs glazing as we've covered material that's admittedly of more primary concern to buyers than sellers, now's the time to stand up, walk around the room, clear your mind and sit back down and concentrate. This is important stuff.

I will assume that most of you still have remaining balances on your mortgage loans. If you own your home free and clear, you may continue to doze and we'll catch you later when we discuss owner financing.

Conventional Loans

Let's say your home's market value is judged to be $150,000. The remaining balance on your 30-year fixed-rate, 8 percent mortgage loan is $100,000. The current interest rate for a comparable loan is 12 percent. You can readily see how it would be to buyer's advantage to take over, or assume, your loan at the better interest rate. You can also readily see how, if you were the lender, you would not be quite as enthusiastic about the assumption.

Prior to the early 1980s it was quite common for conventional mortgage loans to be freely assumable without a requirement for prior lender approval. It was really no big deal because interest rates were comparatively stable, and the original borrower was still quite likely to be on the hook in the event of default. Then came the turbulent years. Interest rates soared and a lot of low-interest loans were being assumed. In response, lenders began to include what is known as an "alienation" or "due on sale" clause in their loan documents, particularly for their fixed-rate loans. If the mortgagor (the borrower) sold the property without prior approval, the mortgagee (the lender) had the right to declare the entire debt due. This feature is now standard on conventional loans and will likely remain so. In most instances, ARMs are assumable because the rate will go up if rates take off.

Conventional Wisdom for Conventional Loans

Whether you list your home or sell it yourself, one of your first steps should be to dig out all of your old loan documents. In most transactions that will include the promissory note you signed and the mortgage or the trust deed that pledges your property as collateral for the loan. These documents may not be comprehensible to the common person, so it would be wise to run them by your attorney if you are not absolutely certain about whether the loan is assumable without prior approval.

If there is a due-on-sale clause—and if your loan has a fixed rate and has been written in the past 10 years, there probably is—you will need to contact your lender in writing and ask under what conditions the loan may be assumed. Assumption can sometimes be an excellent alternative for the buyer and a good sales incentive for you. If your outstanding loan is at 8 percent and prevailing rates are 12 percent, the lender may agree to let it be assumed below the going rate—perhaps 10 percent, plus a modest assumption fee, assuming they judge your buyer to be a good credit risk. They know the property and the loan is seasoned, which means your home is quite likely worth a lot more than the outstanding loan. It's at least worth a try. REALTORS® will quite likely have standard forms for you to fill out to request the information you need from the lender.

FHA Loans

If you have an FHA loan on your home, here are the basics regarding assumability. Loans originated prior to December 1, 1986, qualify for "blind" or simple assumption: the purchaser does not need to meet any type of eligibility requirement or go through any kind of financial qualification analysis. It's as easy as it sounds. Loans taken out between December 1, 1986, and December 15, 1989, are freely assumable after the first two years. After December 15, 1989, borrowers must qualify and meet all FHA guidelines for the specific type of loan they are attempting to assume. No investors may assume these loans, only owner-occupants. It's complicated, and, as they say, it's subject to change. If you have an FHA loan, check with a lender to make certain you have current information.

VA Loans

The rules are not quite as complex for assuming a GI loan. A veteran or nonveteran can assume an existing loan written prior to March 1, 1988, with no qualification requirements. Loans written after March 1, 1988, require the prior approval of the loan holder before the property can be transferred. That approval will be granted only to creditworthy applicants.

The element of future eligibility for other VA loans enters into the equation if you permit your current loan to be assumed. There are several possibilities. You may not have used your entire entitlement when you bought your home. The dollar amount that VA will guarantee (which determines the size of the loan you will be permitted) has risen over the years. You need to get out your original loan documents and find out exactly how much of your entitlement you used. Then run it by a lender that handles VA loans to determine how much you have left and into what size loan that would translate.

You could get your entire eligibility restored for another VA loan if the individual assuming your current loan is a veteran willing to substitute his or her eligibility. When any GI loan is paid off, of course, your eligibility is restored.

Seller Beware!

There's one not-so-minor final item regarding loan assumptions of which you must be aware. As you would probably suspect, lenders like to have as many people as possible on the hook to pay off any given loan. So if they make a loan to you and someone else assumes it, even with the lender's permission, it is entirely possible that you would still be responsible for making up any loss from a future foreclosure. It depends entirely on the technical, legal language of the assumption agreement.

When the property is sold subject to the mortgage, the buyer likely will not be personally obligated to pay the debt. On the other hand, the buyer who purchases the property and assumes and agrees to pay the seller's debt becomes personally obligated for payment of the entire debt. Even then, however, if there were a foreclosure and a deficiency judgment, you might be still held responsible for it. You're confused, right? Now you understand why I say, "Run this one by your attorney."

To make you feel better before we leave this topic, let me give you the best method yet devised of insuring that anyone assuming your loan does not walk away from it and leave you holding the bag. Get a huge amount of money down. If the buyer of your $150,000 house assumes your $100,000 mortgage and gives you $50,000 for your equity, the chances of a default are rare indeed. Even if it did happen and the property was foreclosed upon, there should be enough of a cushion between the outstanding loan balance and the property value to provide a safety net.

On Being a Banker

In the majority of situations in which a home is sold, the buyer goes to the lending institution, gets a loan, and the seller is cashed out. After all the expenses of the sale are deducted (including the payoff of the mortgage loan) the happy homeseller walks away with cold cash and warm memories of the old homestead. However, there are a couple of scenarios in which you, as a seller, could become intimately and personally involved in a more long-term financial relationship with your buyer.

Free and Clear

In our mobile society it is comparatively rare for any of us to live in a home long enough to pay off the mortgage loan. However, if you are the exception to the rule and own your home free and clear, you have the option of being your own banker and financing the sale yourself. Do not exercise this option without the guidance of an experienced real estate attorney and a humorless, hard-nosed accountant.

Horror Stories.   Let me be fair. I have seen situations where individuals have acted as their own bankers, and things have worked out superbly. Instead of making monthly mortgage loan payments, they received them! What could be better than that? On the other hand, I have witnessed, and heard of, some really heart-wrenching stories. Here's one, just to illustrate.

• •

Timber!

An older couple in Oregon owned a nice home on acreage. There was a large, mature stand of Douglas firs on the property. They sold on what is known as a land-sales contract for a minimal down payment to a couple who, they said, reminded them of themselves 40 years earlier. They did no credit check, they hired no attorney, they established no collection escrow account, and they used the contract form the couple provided. They then took off on an extended vacation. When they came back, the timber had been harvested, the house was trashed, and the smooth-talking buyers were long gone. Yes, they did get the place back, stumps and all.

• •

Read My Tips.   You know, of course, that bankers do not have reputations for being sentimental and that the best way to get a loan is to be able to prove conclusively that you don't need the money. That's really not fair. You do have to prove conclusively that there's a high probability (the closer to 100 percent, the better) that you will pay it back.

If you are going to be your own banker then you must start acting like one. Anyone who wants to buy your home should submit a formal loan application on the same form that the local bank uses. Prospective buyers must answer personal questions about where they work, how much money they make, what their assets and debts are, and past bankruptcies. It definitely means doing a formal credit check. A contract should be drawn by your attorney based on input from your accountant and complete with a collection escrow account (for which the buyer pays), into which payments will be made and disbursed to you. If there is no substantial down payment, forget the whole thing.

Taking Back Paper

On loan assumptions there is frequently a gap between the outstanding balance and the equity in the property. Sometimes the gap can be substantial. For example, you may have an assumable $85,000 loan on your $150,000 house. A buyer may have $15,000 to put down, but that would still leave a gap of $50,000. You could agree to take a second mortgage for $50,000 on terms that were mutually agreeable. There may even be a balloon feature, which means that in five years, for example, the total remaining note would be owed to you, thereby requiring the buyer to refinance or come up with the cash in some other way.

If the assumption requires the lender's approval, you can probably count on some assistance, because the lender will likely do some credit and background checking. Be that as it may, it's still imperative that you get legal counsel. You will be in a secondary position to the underlying mortgage (the lender gets its money first if there's a default, and you get what's left, if anything), so you want your position to be as solid as possible. It's also imperative that you get that big pile of cash up front.

Red Flag Checklist and Survival Strategies

1. In gathering your mortgage loan documents you suddenly realize that you have absolutely no idea what your exact mortgage balance is.

Strategy: This is not as uncommon as you might think. You would be surprised at how many blank looks you get from homeowners when you ask for their precise mortgage loan balance. That's an important number to have and to be able to share with buyers. Because the difference between that balance and market value is your equity, it's also an important number for you to have. When you send the letter requesting assumption information, ask for an official balance.

2. You've heard that there is a veterans' loan program sponsored by your state but are having trouble getting information about it.

Strategy: Many states have attractive mortgage loan programs for GIs. They will be administered by an agency of the state government, often titled something like the Department of Veterans' Affairs. Look in the state government section of your telephone directory (in the blue pages) for the information number. Frequently, local lending institutions administer the program. Get descriptive literature along with the phone number for a prospect to call if they're interested.

3. You are told by an acquaintance that when he sold his home he did it with a blind assumption that permitted his buyer to take over his low-interest loan without worrying about qualifying.

Strategy: This scenario happened frequently when due-on-sale clauses first appeared on the scene. Some very creative and very dangerous methods were devised to keep the news from the lending institution that there had been a sale. Not smart at all.

4. You've heard that you could sell your home and take a wraparound mortgage from the buyer, thus not triggering the due-on-sale clause in your mortgage.

Strategy: This was another popular scam. Wraparounds are fine if there is no alienation clause in your original loan agreement. In a wraparound, the seller keeps making the (smaller) original payments on the loan after having sold the property to another individual, from whom (larger) payments are received directly. Get legal advice before you walk down this path.

5. *A friend of yours is a veteran and knows you are planning to sell your home. She's very interested in buying it and knows you've been researching different loan programs. She starts asking you questions about eligibility for a federal VA loan.*

Strategy: I spent more than 25 years in the air force and have been in real estate for over a decade. I still can't keep the eligibility requirements straight. Send her down to the local VA office to get what is called a certificate of eligibility. She will need her DD Form 214, Certificate of Separation. That will clear up the eligibility question and will get her started on the other requirements. There are a lot of them.

6. *You bought your present home new five years ago on an FHA loan. You're about to sell it but have heard horror stories about homeowners who have sold on FHA.*

Strategy: If you have taken reasonable care of your home, you shouldn't need to be worried about permitting a purchaser to buy on FHA. Your original builder had to meet FHA requirements as the home was being built, so it met standards then. Agree to FHA financing and you will increase the marketability of your home substantially.

7. *In discussing the possible assumption of your conventional mortgage loan with a junior officer at the bank, you ask if there isn't some way you could be completely relieved of any responsibility for it. He said, "None that I'm aware of."*

Strategy: The young exec may have been telling you the entire truth—he was not aware of any such method. Had you spoken with a senior officer, it is possible you would have been told about novation, the substitution of new parties to an existing obligation. Lending institutions do not typically give novation marquee exposure, because in the other standard assumptions, the original mortgagor (you) retains some degree of responsibility for the loan. The more the merrier, so to speak.

8.   Somewhere you seem to dimly remember hearing the phrase "prepayment privilege" when you were getting your home loan several years ago.

Strategy: Deep in some loan documents is a clause more commonly (and accurately) known as a prepayment penalty. It simply means that if you prepay your mortgage, you could end up owing the lending institution an added fee. It's not in all loans, and the lender can waive it if it's there. But if you've got a large mortgage with a prepayment penalty, you could be hit for a substantial fee when you pay it off upon selling your house. Check it out early.

9.   You converted your former home into a rental several years ago and are now planning to sell it. You've always done your own taxes and feel confident you can handle this one.

Strategy: Many people who have a single rental property are dumbfounded when they learn what their capital gains tax liability will be when they sell it. You pay taxes on the difference between the depreciated value of the investment and what you sold it for, less some adjustments. The resultant 25 to 35 percent tax hit on that amount will get your attention. At least spring for one consultation session with an accountant before you proceed. Some people decide to exchange that investment property for another more expensive one, thereby deferring taxes.

10.   When you are discussing financing with a potential buyer, he makes it clear that he plans to use the home as a rental although he is telling the lender that he will be an owner-occupant.

Strategy: Although this would primarily be an issue between the buyer and the lender, it is a clear signal that you are working with a dishonest person. Alarm bells should be sounding.

9

$$\cdots \cdots \blacktriangledown \cdots \cdots$$

Hiring Help:
Listing Your Home

True or false: Most people list their homes with a real estate broker rather than trying to sell it themselves. It's a true statement. The exact percentage varies from time to time, depending mainly on whether it's a seller's market or a buyer's market. Real estate industry statistics will typically cite the figure at somewhere between 75 and 85 percent. No matter the precise percentage, even a casual observer can readily see that real estate professionals sell the vast majority of homes in the United States, so we will cover that option first.

Fizzbos Listen Up!

Even if you've decided to enlist in that small but dedicated army of Fizzbos and be one of the few, the proud, and the rich, it is important to understand how the entire process of listing, marketing and title transfer takes place, because no matter who does the selling, certain essential tasks must be accomplished. If a friendly, efficient REALTOR® isn't doing them for you or pointing you in the right direction for guidance from another professional, then they will fall upon your shoulders.

It's also true that many people who initially decide to go the Fizzbo route later change their minds when they find themselves in over their heads.

Employing a Broker

When you list your home, you sign a personal-services employment contract with a real estate broker. The word *contract* is very important. Here's how attorney John Reilly defines it in his book *The Language of Real Estate* (a great basic reference, by the way): "A legally enforceable agreement between competent parties who agree to perform or refrain from performing certain acts for a consideration. In essence, a contract is an enforceable promise."

The key phrase in the definition is "legally enforceable," because if either party to the contract reneges on the terms, the other has legal recourse. Because you are essentially hiring a broker to market your home for you, it's an employment contract. The term *personal services* is used because the contract is considered unique to the broker you hire. As a practical matter, the broker cannot assign or sell your listing to another broker. Ironically, you may never see the broker with whom you have the personal services contract, because you will likely work with a real estate licensee who works for the broker.

To be valid, a contract must include consideration (something of value), which in the case of listings is merely an exchange of promises. You promise to pay the broker a fee (commission) if the broker produces a "ready, willing and able" buyer. The broker promises to do a professional job of locating that highly coveted qualified buyer for your property.

Listings: Getting In

There are all sorts of interesting ways to enter into a contract—some intentional and some unintentional. The important thing about real estate is that you are typically dealing with a commodity with a very high price tag. Because such is the case, and because the family homestead is frequently involved, it is imperative that all the terms of any contract be clear and unambiguous. To prevent misunderstandings, everything should be put in writing, in recognition of which every state has a statute of frauds, patterned after a seventeenth-century English law, which generally requires all contracts relating to the transfer of interests in land to be in writing to be enforceable. In approximately half of the states, such matters specifically include listing agreements.

Even if there were no requirement to put your listing in writing, it would be very unwise not to do so. As movie mogul Samuel Goldwyn is alleged to have said, "An oral contract ain't worth the paper it's written on." It would also be unwise to act in a manner that might lead a third party to conclude that you had entered into a listing agreement.

Listings: There Are Choices

For several years I have taught a yearlong sequence of real estate prelicensing courses to adults at a community college in Oregon. In the first course, "Real Estate Practices," we cover listing agreements. After going over the various types, I ask my students, "How many of you have sold a home through a real estate agent?" Fifteen or twenty students in a class between forty and fifty will typically raise their hands. I then ask, "How many of you were told by the real estate agent that there was more than one kind of listing?" I have yet to have anyone raise a hand. I sense, therefore, that there may not be widespread knowledge about this particular point, and inasmuch as an essential element in establishing a valid contract is informed consent, we will briefly discuss the available options.

Exclusive Right To Sell

This is by far the most common type of listing. Under its terms, no matter who sells your home, the broker earns a commission. Even if you were to locate a buyer on your own and sell it without any help from the agent, you would still owe a commission under this type of listing.

These arrangements understandably motivate real estate brokerage firms to exert the maximum effort possible in marketing your property. They don't have to worry that they will invest a lot of money in promotion and then not recap a commission if you or someone else sell the property. In the normal course of events they will, with your permission, place the listing on the local MLS and offer to cooperate with other brokers on a sale. The typical split is 50–50 between listing and selling offices.

When a real estate agent talks to you about listings, they are referring to these arrangements. Many agents have quite likely never taken any type of listing other than an exclusive right to sell. As a seller, you also need to consider the fact that most MLSs operate in a method that favors these listings and that you will unquestionably generate the most interest in selling your home among the widest audience of real estate agents by signing an exclusive-right-to-sell listing.

Exclusive Agency

In this type of listing, you agree that only one brokerage firm will represent you as your agent. However, you retain the right to sell the property yourself without paying a commission. You can see why a broker might be hesitant to do a big media blitz on your property and then have a buyer contact you directly to buy the property. There is the potential for all sorts of misunderstandings as to who was the procuring cause in listings of this type. Let's say you signed an exclusive agency agreement and the real estate company put a sign in your front yard. A buyer sees the sign and contacts you directly and buys the property. Was the broker, because of the sign, the procuring cause of the sale and therefore owed a commission? In comparison, you see how neat and tidy exclusive-right-to-sell listings are.

Open Listing

In an open listing, you can list your property with several different brokers and still sell it yourself without paying a commission. Could you ever find a broker to take such a listing? Absolutely, if it's the right kind of property. When I was actively selling real estate, the largest commission I ever earned was on an open listing. It was actually my wife's listing, which I sold. It was a large farm that bordered on a stream in an absolutely delightful rural setting near the Oregon coast. I'm not certain how many brokers the owner had it listed with, but there were several, and because she was an ex-REALTOR® she actively tried to sell it herself. We just happened to find the perfect buyers for the property before anyone else did.

If you own a modest home in a typical city subdivision, you are not apt to find brokers enthusiastic about signing on for an open listing. On the other hand, if you own an unusual or particularly desirable property, you might generate a lot of interest.

Net Listing

Let's say you tell a broker, "I want to walk away from this transaction with $100,000. I don't care what you ask for the property or what you sell it for as long as you get me my $100,000 net." I'm sure you can see the potential for misunderstanding and controversy in such an arrangement. These agreements are actually illegal in many states, but you hear of them occasionally—generally when a disgruntled owner sues the broker after the transaction is complete and it is discovered that the broker sold the property for much more money than the owner ever thought possible. Even if these listings are permitted where you live, I strongly recommend against them.

Listing Forms: Boilerplate Specials

In *The Language of Real Estate, boilerplate* is defined as "the standard, fixed language in a contract." Listing forms certainly fall into that category, as do offers to purchase, deeds, mortgages, leases and just about every other document of agreement relating to real estate. There's really nothing wrong with boilerplate language, providing you have read, understood and agreed to the terms contained in the form.

You should also be aware that although the listing document you will be provided may look official and imposing, it is perfectly permissible to cross out, delete or change anything with which you or your attorney do not agree. Of course, the other party to the contract (the broker) must concur. Just don't be intimidated by such phrases as: "Oh, no need to worry about this, it's just standard stuff that appears on all listing forms."

Listings: The Bare Essentials

In most jurisdictions there is no standard, mandated form that must be used for all listings. There are almost an infinite variety of pre-printed forms, and now you can get a customized form just by making the proper entries on a computer. Even in a comparatively small town, it is not unusual for brokers to use several different forms, thereby making your job a bit more complex. Therefore, each time you get a listing presentation, I suggest that you ask for a copy of the listing agreement and that you study it to familiarize yourself with its contents. You should also run it by your attorney. In the great majority of cases, there will be no problems and only minor changes may be necessary, if any at all. However, potential trouble could lurk in a seemingly innocuous legalese sentence, so let someone who understands it explain it to you and make recommendations.

It is truly amazing how one little word or phrase in a legal document can have such profound ramifications. An attorney friend of mine says he wishes he had a dollar for every time a client who has come to him with a problem on a disputed contract has asked him incredulously: "Is **that** what that word means?"

Listings: The Common Elements

Now for a quick rundown on the standard features of most listing agreements, along with some suggested negotiation strategies, when appropriate.

Property Description.   To you it's always been 2819 Serenity Lane, but that's not the official legal description. The agent, attorney or title company will have dug up the correct one, or you can check your deed ahead of time if you're interested.

Names of the Owners.   If you are the sole owner of the property, then only your signature is needed on the listing. However, if there are co-owners, everyone must sign, a particularly complicated state of affairs when there's been a recent divorce and the former spouse is in another location and the communication process is difficult. If there is more than one name on your deed, you need to get all of this sorted out ahead of time and reach a meeting of the minds.

Type of Listing.   You are now well informed and can make your own decisions about which type of listing to choose. In most situations, the exclusive right to sell will likely result in the quickest sale for you at the highest price.

Multiple Listing Authorization.   Unless you want to keep the fact that you are selling your home a secret, I strongly recommend that you authorize the use of MLS.

Brokerage Fee. Typical commissions range from 5 to 7 percent for residential properties, but you will hear over and over again that commissions are negotiable. They are, but if the broker's idea of negotiation is "6 percent, take it or leave it," then you may want to do further interviews. You must consider the impact of the size of your commission on the other agents on MLS. If the standard fare for a property like yours is 6 percent and you can convince a broker to list yours for 4 percent, how do you think cooperating agents will react when they see your house on MLS? Human nature being what it is, they're more likely to want to sell the homes with the higher commissions.

There are also discount brokers, who in essence provide you a menu of services that they will provide. For each activity you choose, there is a charge. If you want to conduct your own open house, for example, you can opt to do that and save money. Is this idea a good deal? Depending on how much work you feel qualified to do, yes. Remember, however, the ability of the cook in the back room is the critical issue—not how great the menu looks. I've also heard and seen some interesting ads by discount brokers. The phrase "no commission, ever" is sometimes used. While that may be true, there is a charge for their services.

Authority To Cooperate with Other Brokers. Because you want the widest exposure possible for your property, you will generally be happy to give your broker the authority to cooperate with other brokers and to share the commission in any way they mutually agree upon.

Should you offer to work with agents representing buyers and have their fee come out of the commission? I don't have a problem with that because in the final analysis it should get your property the most exposure and you should net exactly the same amount. Let's face it. The agents working with the buyers will probably be representing them anyhow, even if they were technically your subagent. Without the buyer's contribution, there won't be any money to pay a commission.

Personal Property or Real Property

When prospective purchasers tour your home, they will assume that such things as the beautiful antique chandelier in the living room stay. If, when they move in, you've replaced it with a two-dollar light fixture from a local garage sale, you can see how they may be unhappy. The general rule is that if it's attached, it is supposed to stay, but there are areas of controversy, and your broker should go over your entire home with you to make certain you are both on the same wavelength. If you plan to include in the sale such appliances as a refrigerator or washer, identify them by make and serial number.

Term of Listing.   This issue is tricky. The listing agent will want as long a period as possible to permit adequate exposure and to justify the expenses of advertising and other marketing activities. Six months (180 days) would probably be the preferred term. You, on the other hand, are likely to be reluctant to sign on for that long, particularly if you've never worked with that agent or brokerage firm before. You may suggest 60 days, along with an offer to renew if you're satisfied. Often, buyers and sellers compromise on 90 to 120 days, although some knowledgeable real estate consumer advocates say no more that 60 days under any circumstances. I'll have some additional suggestions in the "getting out" discussion that follows later in this chapter.

For Sale Sign.   Signs sell real estate, so unless you have some good reason not to permit one in your front yard (there could be some legitimate ones depending upon personal circumstances and preferences), go ahead and authorize it.

Lockbox.   This little device goes on your door with the house key in it. All members of the local MLS will have a key to the box making it convenient for them to show your home, even when you are away. Although the system has been abused, in most circumstances it works out satisfactorily. Some places have high-tech lockboxes, which automatically register the names and firms of all agents who show the house.

You can also have your listing agent keep the key at the brokerage office and check it out for individual showings, or you can permit showings only when you are present to admit people. For maximum potential exposure, the lockbox is best, but if you permit one you must take security precautions and monitor how it is working.

Property Disclosure.   More and more states are requiring that there be formal, written property disclosure statements given to homebuyers before an agreement to purchase is reached. In this instance, even though the basic listing forms may vary, the format of the disclosure statement must be standardized. No matter if property disclosure is mandatory where you live, I highly recommend that you prepare such a form and that you insist that your agent deliver it to anyone who makes a formal offer.

Fair Housing Laws. When you list with a broker, you agree to abide by all local, state and federal fair-housing laws and not to discriminate based on race, creed, color, religion, national origin, sex, familial status or disabilities. This area is volatile, and violating the law— or appearing to—could create more difficulty than you can imagine. Make certain your agent briefs you in detail on local as well as state and federal ground rules.

Carryover Clause. This is also sometimes called an extender provision and will be found in most contracts. It means that if a broker introduces someone to your property during the term of the listing (assuming it's an exclusive right to sell), if that person buys your property within a specified period after the term expires, you still owe a commission. The term can be 60 to 90 days or longer. If it's an exclusive agency, the broker would have had to introduce the prospect to the property. This provision is reasonable, and the reason for it is obvious. A broker could show your property to an unscrupulous buyer who suggests that you wait until the listing expires and then conduct the transaction without paying a commission.

Listings: Getting Out

Entering into a listing agreement is a fairly simple matter. Although there are many important factors to consider relating to the type of listing and its specific provisions, all you really need do is sign the contract. Under certain circumstances, you may not even need to do that.

So how do you get out of the agreement once you've made it? The most common occurrence is the happy-ending scenario—you sell the property. The next most common occurrence is the unhappy-ending scenario—the listing expires without selling it. There are other possibilities. If the broker dies, goes bankrupt or goes out of business, the contract is terminated, because it was, as you recall, a personal-services contract and may not be sold or assigned to another broker. If the property were destroyed, that would obviously end your efforts to sell it— at least in its previous condition.

But now for the sticky wicket issue. What happens if you become disenchanted with the agent's or the brokerage firm's efforts and want to cancel the contract before the expiration date? You would have that right. If the broker agrees with the termination, then there's no problem. Is the broker likely to agree? It will depend upon the circumstances, but in most instances, yes. Real estate brokers do not win friends, influence people and get new clients and customers by suing current ones. However, the broker would probably have that right under the terms of the contract, which could also provide that you reimburse the broker for advertising and other marketing expenses if you terminate early.

If you investigate thoroughly and choose wisely, dissatisfaction will not likely be a problem. But everyone occasionally makes bad judgments and hires the wrong people, and everyone sometimes changes their minds—you might decide that you don't want to sell, or your company might decide not to transfer you after all. To protect yourself, I strongly suggest that you consult your attorney on this particular listing provision. If I listed my home with a broker, I would want the right to cancel without penalty at my discretion. I would be happy to provide the broker with my reasons for canceling in writing.

From a practical, interpersonal standpoint, I suggest the following steps if you are unhappy with the real estate agent servicing your listing. First, talk it over with the agent and explain exactly what it is that displeases you. Second, if the situation does not improve, contact the agent's broker—the person in charge—and explain the reasons for your dissatisfaction. Third, if the situation is still not resolved to your satisfaction, contact your attorney and get guidance on terminating the listing without getting yourself in hot water. Of course, you always have access to the state government agency that supervises and regulates real estate activities. Because they have the authority to do such things as reprimand, fine and revoke licenses, brokers listen carefully when they speak. You will find a roster of state real estate commissions in the Appendix.

• • ▼ •

Red Flag Checklist and Survival Strategies

1. *You have your home on the market as a Fizzbo. An ambitious real estate agent contacts you and asks if it would be all right to show some prospects your home. No mention is made of a formal listing. You agree. He shows it to the same couple several times.*

Strategy: You're headed down a dangerous path fraught with all sorts of unpleasant possibilities. Do not, under any circumstances, let a real estate licensee show your property without a formal, written listing agreement. You could actually be entering into an unintended listing contract by your actions. It's a legal swamp—avoid it.

2. *You ask a real estate agent who is giving you a listing presentation if you can see what an open-listing form looks like so you can compare it to the exclusive-right-to-sell form. The agent looks genuinely surprised and informs you that not only doesn't he have such a form, he's never seen one.*

Strategy: He's probably being honest with you. Training of new agents generally emphasizes the exclusive-right-to-sell listing. He can, however, easily get his hands on one to deliver to you later.

3. *When you ask a real estate agent about an exclusive agency listing, she informs you that her broker does not take them.*

Strategy: That, of course, would be the broker's prerogative. However, very few would arbitrarily reject all exclusive agency listings without considering the individual circumstances. If she's telling the truth, no matter: a competitor down the street would probably be happy to work with you—particularly if it were clear that you would not consider other options.

4. *You've got a $400,000 home in a city where the average price of homes is $150,000. You get faint when you figure what the standard 6 percent commission would be on the sale.*

Strategy: You've got leverage on this one. It generally does not take any more skill, effort or expense to sell an expensive home such as yours. Often it takes less. You might wish to propose something like 6 percent on the first $150,000 and 2 percent on any amount over that. You could use your imagination and come up with other numbers. It's still a great listing.

5. *An agent whom your listing broker tells you is representing a buyer visits your home to preview it before a showing. He is friendly and knowledgeable and asks a lot of questions about your home and your personal circumstances.*

Strategy: Do not tell a buyer's agent anything you would not want to tell the buyer directly. It would be his fiduciary responsibility to his principal, the buyer, to pass on anything you said that would help in negotiations.

6. *You've signed an exclusive-right-to-sell listing agreement and there is a big sign in the front yard. A couple stops in front of your house, rings the doorbell and asks if they can take a quick look.*

Strategy: Somewhere in the fine print of your listing agreement you have probably agreed to refer all inquiries to your agent, both for your protection and for your agent's peace of mind. Politely give the couple a brochure for the house with the agent's phone number on it.

7. *You notice in the listing contract that there is a provision for an automatic 60-day extension on your 90-day listing agreement.*

Strategy: In many states automatic extensions are illegal. If they are legal where you reside, they shouldn't be. Strike this provision out. If you want to extend the listing when it expires, sign an agreement to do so. Based on prior events, you may wish to modify the terms.

8. *You've listed your home for $175,000. Your neighbor, whose fame for having opinions on everything is exceeded only by his willingness to share them, advises, "Better let your broker know what you will actually take, so she can negotiate for you from a position of strength."*

Strategy: May I suggest that you do not know what you will actually take for your home? Price is just one element of an offer, albeit an important one. The terms proposed, including the type of financing and seller concessions, will have an important bearing. My advice? Ignore the advice.

9.   *You've signed an exclusive-right-to-sell 120-day listing agreement with a broker. Shortly after the listing appeared on MLS, another broker visited the property and after inspecting it informed you that you grossly underpriced it.*

Strategy: In some states, the second broker has illegally interfered with a contract, because the obvious motivation would seem to be to get you to cancel your listing and sign with the second broker. Under the REALTOR® Code of Ethics it would likely be considered unprofessional conduct. If you did a thorough job of research, your asking price will be based on solid evidence.

10.   *You have tried to sell your home yourself, but it has turned out to be more than you can handle. Although you have three promising prospects on the line, you decide to sign an exclusive-right-to-sell listing.*

Strategy: Go ahead and sign the listing, but inform the broker in writing of the three names and reserve the right to sell to any of them without paying a commission. This reservation is not uncommon, and the broker should agree, but find out before you formally commit yourself.

10

·····▼·····

Fizzboing:
Just Doing It Yourself

Selling your home yourself could be the best-paying job you ever had. Just so we can deal in round numbers, assume you sell for $200,000 and save a 6 percent commission. That's a cool $12,000. We'll say that not counting the sleep you lost and the time you spent worrying and fretting, you actually put in 60 clock hours at it. We're talking $200 an hour here, which would translate into more than $400,000 per year.

Of course all of this presumes that you successfully sell your home. Otherwise you do all of that work for nothing and still have a large unsolved problem on your hands. By now, you've got a good, solid foundation in the basic fundamentals of successful homeselling. We'll now cover important information you'll need to have to get your Fizzboing plan off the ground. But first, a safety briefing from your flight attendant.

Practicing Safe Selling

If you list your home, you will probably be given a few tips on common-sense safety procedures by your agent. It's an unfortunate fact of contemporary life that there is an alarming and increasing number of predators among us. If you're selling on your own you need to be particularly alert, because you will not have that buffer between you and the prospects.

Although everything will probably be peaceful, you know the Boy Scout motto.

• •

"Be Prepared" Fizzbo Safety Checklist

1. Do not let anyone you do not know just stop by and enter your house. Show by appointment only.

2. When making appointments, get the name and telephone number of the prospects.

3. Do your best to have at least two people on hand when the home is shown—if necessary, have a neighbor drop over.

4. Never show your property at night.

5. If you are home alone and someone rings the doorbell, do not open the door until you know who it is and you feel comfortable.

6. Secure all valuables in your house. Take everything breakable and vulnerable off the shelves or at least out of reach.

7. Do not leave a key under the doormat or anywhere else easily accessible.

8. Communicate with your neighbors so they know your plans and activities and would be able to spot any unusual activities.

9. Be attentive to suspicious mannerisms exhibited by any visitors.

10. Con artists can be incredibly charming. Keep everything on a strictly business basis and share no confidences with strangers.

• •

Promoting Your Product

You've got a great product, you've priced it right and packaged it well, and you've vowed to practice safe selling. You're ready to deal. This could be the easiest part of the entire undertaking or it could be the most difficult and frustrating. Let's take easy first.

• •

Fizzbo Fantasy

Your home has secret admirers who have worshiped it from afar for years. We'll call them the Fredstroms, an affluent retired druggist and his schoolteacher wife. They look at your place longingly each day as they drive by in their car heading for the market, never daring to dream that someday you would offer it for sale. The very moment you are pounding your "for sale by owner" sign into the ground, they happen to be passing by. They screech to a halt, run to your side, rip the sign out of the ground, and scream in unison: "We'll take it! Price is no object! We'll pay cash! When can we move in?"

Although I've embellished just slightly, things do sometimes happen almost exactly that way. The problem is that you can't count on it, so your challenge is to get the word to as many potential buyers as possible.

• •

Marketing Folder

We've already suggested that you gather up certain important documents to show your serious prospects. It would probably be wise to get a hard-cover ringed binder to hold these documents neatly in place. Keep in mind as you are put this binder together that it will serve as a marketing tool. Let's say you had three real estate agents come by and each gave you a competitive market analysis. Two were similar and suggested a market value close to your asking price. There would be nothing wrong with including these documents. On the other hand, if one was somewhat lower, I doubt you would be faulted for not including it. The same could be said for an inspection report that pointed out a problem you've since corrected. If your roof leaked at one time and you've since gotten a new one, there would be no purpose served by including the old inspection report.

Here are some of the items that you may want to include in your folder: a blank offer-to-purchase form you had reviewed by your attorney; if it's assumable, a fact sheet showing the basics of your mortgage loan, including the balance; a record of survey of the grounds if you have one; a list of the personal property that stays, if any; the formal inspection report; records of major improvements; utility records; a map of the property identifying shrubs and trees by name; photos of the property at different times of the year; any deed restrictions; and maybe even a copy of your deed to impress folks that you know what one is and can locate it.

Flyer

If things go according to plan, you will have a lot of people coming by to look at your home. They will likely have looked at many other homes and after a while it's hard to keep track of things. I recommend that you have a one-page flyer prepared describing your home. A nice picture of it would make it more memorable, and you should include at least a rough sketch of the floor plan, including room sizes, as well as of the lot. On the reverse you could include the sketch you made of the local area showing distances from your home to major facilities.

Remarkable products can be generated on computers these days, so if you have that capability you can prepare your own flyer. If not, contact a local graphics or printing company that specializes in jobs like that and get them to do it for you. After it's prepared, it's comparatively inexpensive to have copies run off. Get a supply for your home and, assuming the interpersonal relationships are tolerable, give one to each of your neighbors. One of them may know someone who would love to move in. People often set up a box of flyers near or on the For Sale sign so people driving by can pick one up (make sure it's weatherproof so everything doesn't get soggy).

Here's a very important caution: it's always wise to tell the truth; it's critical when you put something in writing. If you're not sure what the square footage is of your house, don't guess. If your flyer says, "Spacious 3,000-square-foot English Tudor" and the house is actually 2,200 square feet, guess what could end up as exhibit one when you are sued for misrepresentation?

Mortgage Rate Sheet

Whether you're selling in a buyer's market or a seller's market, financing can frequently be the deciding factor in a purchase decision.

You want to get up to date on who's making loans and on what terms. It would be wise to reduce the results of your research to one document, called a rate sheet, and have it available at your home. If you are informed on financing, you will reduce buyer anxiety and bolster confidence in your ability to handle the sale on your own.

It won't be that difficult for you to get mortgage rates. Contact at least two of the more prominent lending institutions in town and ask for any guidance they can give you about selling your home. You will probably receive a royal reception, because there's a good chance that if you're impressed you will attempt to send purchasers to that lender. Remember with whom you talked so you can call back with questions as they arise and refer a buyer to a specific person.

Also locate what is known as a mortgage broker. Mortgage brokers do not make loans, but they represent several lenders and will have a good grasp of the range of options open to a purchaser. It typically does not cost the borrower anything to work with a broker because brokers usually receive a fee from the lender with whom they place the loan. If the mortgage broker has a rate sheet displaying the local mortgage menu, you can probably take along a supply for your home. If you can't locate a rate sheet in this manner, check the real estate section in the nearest large metropolitan newspaper (generally in the Sunday edition). Newspapers frequently have an extensive display of mortgage rates in the area and may even have toll-free telephone numbers so that you can get up-to-date quotes around the clock.

For Sale Sign

I hope you are convinced of the benefits of putting a For Sale sign in your front yard. I recognize that there may be some instances where signs aren't appropriate, but they are effective. Exactly what percentage of actual sales results directly from For Sale signs is difficult to accurately determine, but there's no debate about their usefulness as a marketing tool.

Your sign should be large and colorful enough to attract attention. I strongly recommend you have it professionally done with printing on both sides so it can be read from either direction. Your phone number should appear in large print, because that's what people will write down. Also prominently featured should be the phrase "by appointment only."

I'll let you in on a little trade secret. There is a direct, positive correlation between the quality of a Fizzbo's For Sale sign and the Fizzbo's commitment to go it alone. In other words, if you see a cardboard "for sale by owner" sign that was purchased at the local variety store, tacked to a piece of warped plywood barely standing up in the yard, you've likely got a Fizzbo who is not really committed and probably not very well informed. These people will probably throw in the towel at the first sign of distress or difficulty and list their properties. If you go the tacky-sign route, expect numerous calls from real estate agents anxious to test your mettle and list your property. Also expect certain buyers, skilled in the ability to read nonverbal signals, to conclude that you are naive and inexperienced in the facts of business life.

Newspaper Ads

Advertising your home in your local paper is a must. Your first chore will be to become an avid reader of the real estate section. Put yourself in a buyer's position. Which ads catch your attention (in a positive way), and why? Jot down terms and phrases that are effective and adapt them to your ad.

Fizzbos often start their ads with "For Sale by Owner" or "By Owner." I can't really argue with that, because that is an important part of the message. I would certainly include it somewhere, if not at the start. In all states with which I am familiar, real estate brokers must indicate in any ad that they are licensed agents. The requirement even applies when selling their own homes. That's designed to protect consumers by putting them on notice that they will be working with a professional who has superior knowledge. In other words, buyer beware. On the other hand, when you announce prominently that you are a Fizzbo you lay claim to amateur status. Your goal, of course, is to be as knowledgeable as the pro.

What's the single most important factor in the homebuying decision? You know—location. If you live in a desirable area, that should be part of your lead sentence, in bold type. Let's say you live in a neighborhood known as Hillcrest Heights. Except for the million-dollar mansions down by the lake, it's considered to be the most desirable neighborhood in the area. A logical lead sentence or head for your classified ad might read, "Hillcrest Heights—By Owner."

You want to then maintain interest and focus the message as directly as possible to interested and qualified buyers. For example, if you've got a colonial-style home, "classic colonial" would catch readers' eyes. Then, in as little additional copy as possible, describe the outstanding features of your home, including those that are unique or particularly desirable, as well as the number of bedrooms and baths.

Should you include the price in your ad? Unless you want a lot of calls from people who love what you've said about your home but couldn't possibly afford it, yes. Do not include qualifiers, such as. "asking $145,000." That's shorthand for "That's what I'm asking, but I'll take a lot less." If your personal circumstances border on the desperate and you really wish to stir up the sharks, share with the reading public your real motivation for selling. Just a slight alteration in your ad will do it. "For sale by bankrupt owner," for example, would almost certainly guarantee you an incredible response. Have your shark repellent handy.

How about your address? I say yes, but make certain you also include "by appointment only." Brokers typically do not include addresses in their ads because they want prospects to call their offices. That way, they can do some preliminary prequalification and secure an appointment to show the home, thereby insuring that the caller does not head off to another broker to buy the property. Even serious and motivated buyers who call about specific homes generally end up purchasing something else, so agents can steer prospects to other listed homes. But you don't care if they buy a different house: you've only got one home to sell, and the more you can do to get it exposure, the better. The downside? You will get a lot of people driving slowly by your home. And despite the "by appointment only" in your ad and on your sign, some may stop and knock on your door. Again, courteous and firm, but no wavering: "by appointment only." No one in the house without an appointment, except at an open house.

Some newspapers have special arrangements in which for a modest fee they will take a photo of your home to accompany the ad. If your place takes a nice picture, it could be effective.

There are clever ways of putting the best spin on a negative factor. One ad I saw said, "Oversize one-car garage." Be realistic, however, and remember that no matter how enticing you make your home sound, people will come over and take a look. If you live under the off-ramp of the busiest freeway in the state and describe that as "convenient to transportation," it may generate visits but it won't do much to enhance your credibility.

Finally, if you don't want to get calls from real estate brokers, you can add, "no agents," but that phrase may not deter them all. I'll have guidance for you on that topic shortly.

"Homes" Magazines

"For Sale By Owner" magazines are becoming quite popular. For a fee you can display a picture of your home along with a description. Depending upon cost and circulation, I think these publications represent a wise investment. A step beyond would be a television ad if there's such a program in your area. The more high-tech you go, of course, the more money it will cost you. If you have an expensive home with comparatively few qualified buyers in the wings, you may wish to pull out all the stops. There are even computer networks that are getting into the game.

Multiple Listing Services

It may be possible for you to get your home listed on the local MLS, either through a discount broker or for a set fee. Unfortunately, you would have to sign an agreement that if someone on the MLS sold it, you would owe them a brokerage fee—perhaps 3 percent of the sales price. Your total cost may end up less than a traditional listing fee, but probably not by much.

Open Houses

Holding a formal open house is a nuisance, and there is some question among real estate brokers about whether it is really an effective marketing strategy. There are many open houses because sellers expect them. Even though it's comparatively rare for an open house to result in a direct and immediate sale for the home being held open, it does happen occasionally, and (more importantly) it puts the broker in contact with a lot of people who may be potential purchasers for other houses.

If I were putting my own home on the market, I think I would do the best job I could of getting exposure through newspaper ads and such. Then I would see what kind of a response I received. If I hadn't located a solid buyer within two or three weeks, I would hold the open house.

You will have already done most of the drudgery just to get your home ready to put on the market, but when you start showing it or holding it open, there are some additional steps you need to take. First, it must be spick-and-span, with no odors that could offend. To keep the air breathable, it would be good to have a no-smoking sign posted near the front door. If someone lights up anyway, simply say something like, "I'm sorry, but I'm allergic to tobacco smoke." It's unlikely that the smoker will demand to see a doctor's certificate. Of course, if you are a smoker or do not wish to discourage others from smoking, simply have ashtrays conveniently located all over the house. Understand, however, that you will alienate a large group of buyers who will lose interest and potentially leave immediately.

As a result of your "clean it up and move it out" campaign, your home will be tidy and uncluttered. Open all the drapes and turn on as many lights as practical. If it's winter, a nice fire in the fireplace adds a homey touch. Make certain it's not the first time you've used it in a couple of years, however, because you could have problems with the chimney. If it's the wet season, you may want to put plastic runners over your carpet.

When I sold real estate actively, the company for which I worked was a member of a national franchise. They had an effective method of calling attention to a home's noteworthy attributes—small cardboard signs that had "Special Feature" printed on the top with a description of the object in question. We would place the signs at the appropriate locations. You could accomplish the same thing with a magic marker and some firm white cardboard. If there are items such as washers or dryers that are not included in the sale, but are negotiable, it would be good to have a sign pointing them out. Even if you think you would just as soon leave them as part of the deal, it's probably wise to save that as a negotiating tool. If you give them away up front, then the focus will be on other concessions.

You will want to place an ad in the local paper a couple of days ahead of the open house with clear directions to get there. On the day of the open house you will want to place "open house" signs with arrows at strategic locations around your neighborhood. (I told you holding open houses was a royal pain.) To do the job right there should be at least two people available to greet guests and move around the house answering questions. If there are children or pets in the household, do your best to find them temporary shelter elsewhere. You want your total attention to be on the job at hand. If you have inside four legged pets, relegate them to the back forty or a cozy, tied up corner in the garage. Some dogs, in particular, get very protective when strangers show up while others get embarrassingly friendly or obnoxiously amorous.

As your guests arrive, greet them, introduce yourself and ask them to sign a guest register. This may sound a little hokey, but for security reasons and for follow up it is a good practice. After the guests sign in you should accompany them to the kitchen, where you should have your flyers and your marketing folder on a counter. How much time you can spend with each visitor will depend on how many of them there are, but either you or your partner should greet each newcomer at the door.

Don't crowd your visitors and don't feel obligated to take them from room to room making such obvious announcements as, "This is the living room." I would suggest that you try to engage each in conversation to get to know them. You might start with, "Do you live here in town?" At the start, take the focus away from the house and try to achieve rapport. If the vibes are good, you can follow with questions that could reveal employment status, qualification and seriousness of intent. If people like and trust you they are more apt to feel comfortable in doing business with you. That you are likeable and trustworthy will come across in the conversation. You, naturally, will be doing some character assessment of your own. It will also be clear that you are an informed, no nonsense seller. If your visitors are uncommunicative, don't press them, but let them know you will be available to answer any questions.

After the open house, you should call each visitor. Don't appear overly anxious, but ask them if any questions occurred to them after they left. It's possible that you will get valuable feedback on things that turned them off, or they may just be too timid to call you with an important question.

Dealing With the Dealers

When you publicly declare your official Fizzbo status, you will attract a lot of attention—from real estate agents. You are, after all, a commission ready to happen if you can just be convinced that you would be better off listing.

You will need to decide early whether you want to hear what agents have to say. If you are well informed, organized, confident, open minded and tolerant I suggest you listen to them. Be forewarned, however, that you're likely to hear some persuasive arguments. A few examples:

Buyers in Waiting

Most successful real estate agents have a list of qualified buyers for whom they are on the lookout for just the right home. There are times when that list is longer than others, but an active, productive agent will always have some good, solid prospects. Each day they check the new listings that come out on the local MLS, because that's the most likely source. However, they also check Fizzbos.

• •

"I've Got a Buyer . . . Really"

Let's say that I'm working with the Channings, a couple looking for an established, low-maintenance, three-bedroom two-bath home in the popular Sundance development. They are willing to pay no more than $225,000, although they could easily go higher. You put your home on the market and your ad begins, "By Owner: Classy English Tudor in Sundance. $230,000."

I call you and start our conversation by identifying myself as a REALTOR®. I explain the situation and ask if you would consider letting me come over to look at the inside of your home to see if it might be right for the Channings.

Your first question to me is likely to be, "If they like it and buy it, how much would you charge me?" There are several possible answers. I could say, "Nothing, because I am the agent of the buyers and they will pay my fee." Or I could say, "I would like to get a one-party listing. If the Channings buy your property, our brokerage fee would be 6 percent." A savvy seller might say, "Because you wouldn't be splitting your commission with another broker, how about 3 percent?" You could well strike a deal, because commissions are negotiable and most agents work on the sound business philosophy that something is better than nothing.

Should you agree to let me take a look at your home? Absolutely. What have you got to lose? You still have to agree to any offer that's presented. It is entirely possible that I can show you how you would actually net more out of the Channing transaction than you would if you sold it yourself—like if I got you a full-price offer. Remember, the size of the check you walk away with is the only thing that matters. If I save you work and I can get you as much or more money, what's not to like about that?

On the other hand, what if you begin to strongly suspect that I've fabricated the whole shabby story just to get my pushy foot in the door? Just listen politely (you could learn something that would help you in your selling efforts), thank me for coming over, and tell me you're not interested in my services.

• •

"Let Me Help You . . . No Charge"

When you had real estate agents give their listing presentations to help you establish your asking price, you probably got a lot of free advice in other areas as well. As an avowed Fizzbo you will get many other offers—at no cost or obligation to you. Although I firmly believe that there's no such thing as a free lunch, you get what you pay for, and (my favorite) the only free cheese is in the mousetrap, there are exceptions to every rule. This is one of them.

You could quite possibly get a letter in the mail from a real estate agent offering you a free "For Sale By Owner Kit" which would contain advice on everything from pricing your home to having a smooth closing. "Why is she being so nice to me?" you may ask. Simple. It's great business. You could turn out to be one of the many Fizzbos who quickly tires of playing real estate agent and lists—probably with that person who was so helpful. Or you could sell successfully and be so grateful that you can't stop talking about what a truly dedicated, selfless real estate agent you know. Good business and good feelings both ways.

Let Me Confuse You

It's difficult to explain the homeselling process without making it sound incredibly complex, even when you're trying not to. Think what it would sound like if someone were intentionally trying to confuse you. Why would anyone want to do that? Perhaps to push you over the edge and induce you to throw up your hands and proclaim, "Save me from all this—list my home!"

Let Me Scare You

A lot of scary things can happen to a home. For example, little wood-eating critters might start chomping away at critical supporting beams. If a visiting agent bent down, picked up what looked like a little pile of freshly chewed sawdust and exclaimed, "Looks as though you have a carpenter-ant infestation," would it shake your confidence in your ability to manage your homeselling venture yourself? The agent might have just done you a valuable favor by picking up something everyone else had overlooked, but it wouldn't be a bad idea to get a second opinion before you lose your cool and list.

The End Game

All of this effort is designed to do one thing—generate an official, written offer to purchase. All offers are not created equal, however, so the next chapter will provide guidance about how to discriminate between the good, the bad and the ugly.

Red Flag Checklist and Survival Strategies

1.   In discussing what type of For Sale sign to put in your front yard, your mate says, "Are you sure we want to put a sign out there? We're likely to get a lot of people stopping by unexpectedly."

Strategy: Even though you have "by appointment only" on the sign, some folks may still come to the door unannounced. You simply have to be firm. Polite, but firm. Appointment only, when you are prepared to show.

2.   You have indicated "no agents" in your ad, but you immediately get a call from a broker. When challenged, he responds, "Oh, I'm calling as an investor, not an agent."

Strategy: This may or may not be legitimate. It's an approach some agents use to get inside and meet you. They rationalize their actions on the basis that if it were truly a steal they might possibly buy it. I would only respond positively if I were getting short on visitors and was considering listing anyhow. You can get a pretty good indication about the sincerity factor by how much tap dancing the agent does around the investment issue.

3.   In attending open houses held by real estate companies, you notice that there are often plates of cookies and other goodies placed around the homes and that the smell of freshly baked bread seems to permeate the places.

Strategy: It's natural that you will want to make a good impression on visitors and make them feel at home. However, I would not suggest the hot-cookie and fresh-bread routine, because it could give the impression that you're trying a bit too hard and that there might be something from which you would like to divert attention. Friendly but businesslike would be my suggestion.

4.   You are conducting your open house by yourself. You are alone when a couple arrives. You are engaged with one of them in a friendly, extended conversation when you notice that the other one is nowhere to be seen.

Strategy: This could be perfectly innocent or a disturbing warning sign of a standard routine for con artists. You talk to one while the other looks for any valuables that could be picked up and placed in a purse or in a coat pocket. An even scarier scenario is that they may see so many valuable objects lying around that they would schedule an unannounced return while you were away from the house. Always try to have at least two people at an open house. Keep everyone under as friendly surveillance as possible and be attentive for suspicious behavior.

5.   A real estate agent who is looking at your home (with your approval, of course) stops at your water heater, looks perplexed and says, "Uh oh, galvanic corrosion."

Strategy: If, in fact, your hot water heater has contracted the deadly condition, you need to get it replaced or repaired. But first, call your plumber to come take a look. It may be nothing. Real estate agents can sometimes be alarmists.

6. *When composing your newspaper ad for your home you start with "Perfect for Retired Couple."*

Strategy: If you advertise your home, a number of phrases are prohibited by federal fair-housing laws. Anything that would indicate possible discrimination based on race, color, sex, familial status, handicap, religion or national origin is not allowed. Your ad could discriminate against children. The newspaper people will have guidelines for you.

7. *You have a large, multicolored "for sale" sign made at considerable expense. The day you put it up, your helpful neighborhood proctor calls to ask if you're aware of the local sign ordinances.*

Strategy: There are, in fact, some communities that regulate the signs that may be placed in your yard. There are also restrictions in certain subdivisions that do the same thing. Better check everything out before you spend your money.

8. *A man calls and makes an appointment to view your home. He gives his name but seems reluctant to give you his phone number.*

Strategy: You can justify needing his phone number because you may need to call him before he arrives if you are unable to keep the appointment for some reason. If he becomes really evasive, I would be suspicious.

9. *There are CC&Rs that apply to the neighborhood in which your home is located. You saw them when you first moved in but cannot locate a copy.*

Strategy: You should include this document in your marketing folder, because CC&Rs often limit a homeowner's rights. Any such restrictions will be recorded and available at your local public documents agency. If you have a title company, it can get you a copy, as could an attorney or a real estate agent.

10.   *You've never had a formal survey of your property, but it's always seemed from reading the plat map that your fence extends into the back part of your neighbor's lot.*

Strategy: It would be money well spent to have a survey done and the boundaries of your property clearly marked. If your fence is on your neighbor's land, it could eventually result in a controversy for the person who bought your home.

11

······▼······

Offers You Can't—
and Can—Refuse

Talk is cheap, and when it relates to real estate transactions it is rarely binding upon the talkers. If it involves the sale of your home, everything must be agreed upon in writing by both the offeror (the buyer) and the offeree (you). Once that meeting of the minds is reached, you have a contract, which is legally enforceable by either party. It's the point in your homeselling adventure when things get serious.

Legal Stuff

If you have pursued your venture to this point without benefit of legal counsel, it's time to abandon your lonely ranger status and seek professional help. At the very minimum, you will want an experienced real estate attorney to review any offer to purchase before you sign it. One more time—BEFORE you sign it. That goes whether you are working with the best real estate agent in the history of the universe or doing it entirely on your own.

Beware of the Guardhouse Lawyers

Military troops use the term *guardhouse lawyers* to refer to people who know just enough about the military justice system to make them dangerous. The real problem is that almost all of them are quite anxious to share their views with anyone who will listen and some of them are extremely convincing. It should be a tip off for you that guardhouse lawyers got their name by the fact that they are frequently encountered in the guardhouse, which is a holding facility for those awaiting court martial. Where would you encounter these often well-meaning but potentially dangerous folks in a real estate transaction? Friends, relatives, strangers on just about any street corner and even real estate agents. Most oldtimers in the business have learned their lessons the hard way and are sparing with any comments that could be construed as legal advice. On rare occasions, though, some who have not yet graduated from the school of hard knocks will stray slightly over the line. How do you protect yourself? By being informed and by consulting your real lawyer.

Keep in mind as you read this chapter that I am not attempting to play guardhouse lawyer. Even if I were an attorney, which I am not, it would be impossible to offer guidance that would apply in all situations in all parts of the country. Although the basic process is the same everywhere and the end result identical, there are marked differences in procedure, terminology, law and custom.

Promises, Promises

Two of the most important contracts in real estate are listing agreements, which we discussed in Chapter 8, and the offers to purchase (also known as real estate sales contracts, binders, and earnest money agreements). To be valid, offers to purchase must meet certain minimum requirements. Here are a few of the more important ones and a few practical suggestions in each area.

Competent Parties. If your potential buyer looks remarkably young, investigate further. A minor, for example, could agree to buy your property and do it legally but would probably have the option of backing out (voiding the contract). I also once worked with an individual who was not legally capable of entering into a contract because he was not mentally competent. He acted quite informed and just as rational as most of my other customers, but imagine my surprise when he informed me that his guardian would have to approve all the paperwork. There are generally signs that will tip you off—but not always. If there is any doubt, you can ask some diplomatic questions, such as, "Will anyone else be involved in the decision to buy the house?"

Writing.   Theoretically, you could agree to sell your home on a handshake, and if you transferred the property correctly and both parties remained agreeable, the transaction would be entirely legal. To be enforceable, however, it would have to be in writing.

Here are some cautions. Forms vary widely. In most localities, almost any standard document is acceptable, assuming it is filled out properly and all legal niceties are observed. Even under the best of circumstances, however, these documents are difficult for laypeople to understand. Unfortunately, the best of circumstances rarely prevail. Both listing and sales-contract forms quite often border on the incomprehensible, and they commonly run several pages of very small print and very big words. Every time a new issue surfaces or controversy arises, the next form out contains another clause or two designed to cover the situation.

If you are represented by a real estate agent, ask for copies of the most common forms used locally. Read them over carefully and ask questions, both of your agent and of your attorney if it's a particularly murky point. As we discussed previously, if you are on your own, you will have secured an offer form and will have it available for purchasers to review.

There's another important reason for approaching any standard real estate contract form with great caution. At one time they were generally believed to be written to favor sellers. If in fact such were ever the case, it is no longer. Most recent provisions, such as property disclosure and agency disclosure, are designed primarily to protect the buyer's rights. Remember also who designs these forms—representatives of the real estate profession. You should not be surprised, therefore, to find that some of the requirements are designed to insulate real estate professionals from liability. In most cases, these diverse interests work together for the good of all, but wouldn't it be comforting to have an attorney who represents your interests only to look everything over?

A lot of talk will precede any formal offer to purchase. Many issues will be discussed, and some tentative agreements will perhaps be reached. How that talk gets translated into writing is critical. People hear and say things from their own frame of reference and seemingly quite routine matters can be seriously misunderstood. For example, let's say you are pretty sure you remember everyone agreeing to a closing and possession date of June 1. If, when the offer to purchase is submitted in writing, that date is July 1 and you sign off on it, then the written document prevails. The moral: read everything carefully to insure that the written word reflects the spoken word. Once that contract is entered into, nothing is negotiable. Remember also that although the forms look imposing, changes can be made by striking out and adding phrases or even clauses.

Meeting of the Minds.   A definite offer must be made, and the acceptance must be clear and unambiguous. It's also important to understand the sequencing of the offer and acceptance for a meeting of the minds to occur. When an offer to buy your house is made, it's simply that—an offer. It can be withdrawn at any time prior to your acceptance. You can accept or reject any offer. Of course, you could also ignore an offer entirely, but because offers almost invariably come with a time limit, your inaction would be a rejection. If you make any changes, however minor, it's the same as a rejection and is in essence a counteroffer. If you agree to an offer and the person making the offer has been informed of that acceptance, you have a meeting of the minds—a contract.

Consideration.   Usually something of value, in a real estate offer to purchase it is typically the promise to pay a certain purchase price in money in exchange for the promise to deliver a deed.

Signature.   To be bound by a contract, a person must sign it. Is that a problem in a homeselling situation? It could be. Let's say you show your house to a man who informs you that he is in town on a house-hunting trip for himself and his wife. Presuming they plan to take title together, you need both signatures. Has a husband ever made a decision that his wife may not go along with? Rarely, but it would be good to get both the John and Jane Hancock signatures before you get too excited.

Firing for Record

Now that you have the framework within which to understand the barrage of offers you will be receiving, let's take a look at some of the specific items about which you will have to make judgments.

Whether you have a real estate agent representing you, you will make the final decisions. The forms will differ, but the essentials generally are as follows:

Price

Remember that price is only one facet of the offer, albeit a very important one. Here's an example. You are asking $200,000 for your home and have informed anyone who will listen that you won't take a penny less. You do, in fact, get a full-price offer with the proposal that you pay two points for the buyer's loan fee. That's $4,000, but you did get a full-price offer. The bottom line is that you could have accepted a $196,000 offer and netted the same amount.

The proposed terms of the offer as well as the caliber of the person making it should also affect your decision. A full-price offer from shaky buyers with a lot of contingencies would be much less desirable than a somewhat lesser offer made with a clean cash-out proposal by a blue-chip buyer.

Terms

Terms generally means, "How are you going to pay for it?" Terms can range from an all cash offer to a mortgage assumption to complete owner financing. "The devil is in the details," as they say, so make certain you understand all the terms completely and that you can live with them. We'll expand on this discussion later in this chapter.

Earnest Money Deposit

Throwing some money in the pot up front is supposed to demonstrate seriousness of purpose and a commitment. It's not a legal requirement to form a valid contract, but it's almost always done, and I wouldn't enter into a contract to sell my home without one.

How much is enough? The amount varies widely in different parts of the country. One to three percent of the purchase price is sometimes quoted as an appropriate amount. Rarely would a deposit exceed 10 percent. Your goal, of course, would be to get as much as possible, while the buyer's objective would be to demonstrate good intentions without tying up a lot of money. If you are working with a broker, the earnest money will likely be deposited in a neutral escrow or broker's trust account. If you are on your own, it will make the buyer feel safer if you have the money deposited in an escrow account or with your attorney. Make arrangements ahead of time so you don't fumble for an answer when the buyer asks you what you plan to do with the check.

You should also be aware that there are different forms of earnest money. It is quite common for buyers to execute a promissory note for the amount, redeemable upon acceptance of the offer. That's no problem, as long as you are aware of the fact that it is a promissory note. Good business practice would dictate that you wait until the promissory note is redeemed by a check or other immediately negotiable instrument before you go further.

Additional Deposit

There are times when a fairly modest initial earnest-money deposit is accompanied by a proposal to deposit a more substantial amount after the offer has been accepted. If you got a proposal with what you thought was not enough earnest money, you might suggest this approach. If you are selling yourself and you are working with inexperienced buyers, make certain they know that the earnest-money deposit goes toward their purchase price—people sometimes believe it's an extra charge.

Possession

In the majority of home sales, the buyers move in as soon as or shortly after the transaction officially closes. In some instances, however, they may request possession prior to close. Typically, they would pay a per-day rental rate to the seller until close. Use any excuse, but don't agree to this procedure. Renters tend to find all sorts of little problems that they expect owners to take care of prior to close. If they were the official owners they would likely make the repairs themselves. If for some reason you do agree to let the new owner move in before closing, make certain that both you and the buyers understand the insurance and liability ramifications. What happens if the property burns down prior to close? Whose insurance company is responsible? What happens if the buyers' child finds a can of paint you inadvertently left behind and uses it on a playmate? I don't like any of these possibilities. Keep it clean and neat. You pay the money, you get the deed, you move in.

Personal Property

We mentioned the issue of personal property briefly in Chapter 9 when we discussed the formal listing agreement you would complete if you hired a broker, and in Chapter 10 when we covered Fizzboing. The topic deserves some additional emphasis at this point to insure that you have a good handle on it before you receive an offer to purchase.

All property is classified as either real or personal. Things that are tangible and movable are personal property. If you want to sell personal property, you do so with a bill of sale. Real property, on the other hand, includes the earth's surface, the air above and the ground below, as well as all buildings, structures and other improvements permanently attached. It also includes intangible rights that go with the property, such as the ability to sell it or encumber it with a loan. When you sell real property, you do so with a deed.

Why should you be interested in this academic discussion? Because nasty disputes often arise in real estate transactions as to what was real property and what was personal. When a person buys a house, the real property stays, but the personal property goes. Here's a practical example. You have a nice microwave oven that sits on your kitchen countertop. It just plugs in. When you sell your home, you may take it with you if you want. It's personal property. Suppose, however, that the microwave is housed in a cabinet that was built specifically for it and is an integral part of your cooking arrangement. If you took it out, you would need to do some patching. In most people's eyes, that microwave would be considered real property and should stay as part of the purchase price of the house. I'm sure you can see the makings of some major misunderstandings here.

My advice on personal property is to decide early what stays and what goes and make it clear to purchasers. Leave objects that add to the appearance of the house, for example, window coverings. If there are major items you do not particularly want to take with you, such as refrigerators and washers and dryers, I would indicate that they are negotiable. If you are working with first-time buyers, in particular, being willing to throw in a washer and dryer might be just the added incentive that would seal the deal.

Contingencies

Each item we've discussed to this point will simply be a matter of negotiation between you and the buyer. The buyer proposes and you either approve and move on or you disapprove and negotiate an agreement or the whole process stops. Contingencies are different, and they will almost always be an integral part of an offer to purchase real estate. A contingency is simply an event that must happen before the contract is binding. If the event does not happen, the buyer is not obligated to buy the property and gets back any earnest-money deposit. The most common example is that the transaction would depend on the buyer getting financing. We'll discuss this subject further in a moment.

There are several important things to keep in mind regarding contingencies. Perhaps the most important is that a buyer will tie up your property while the contingencies are being satisfied. That being the case, any contingency should be stated precisely and should include a specific time frame within which each must be completed. Here are some of the most common contingencies.

Title.   In every offer to purchase form I've ever seen, there is a standard clause that makes being able to deliver good title a contingency of the sale. That's understandable and will be no problem for you if you've had the preliminary title search completed. In most transactions, the seller pays for title insurance for the property, which simply means that the title is insured as of the date of the sale against defects and certain claims. You want to avoid surprises that surface at the last moment.

Financing.   If your buyers have been prequalified or preapproved for a loan, this contingency may not be critical, but historically it has proved one of the most troublesome. If the offer says something like, "Contingent upon the purchaser being able to secure acceptable financing," you've given the buyer a big stick. It would be much better to be specific: "Contingent upon purchasers being able to secure a first mortgage in the amount of $175,000 at a fixed interest rate not to exceed 10 percent, for a term no less than 30 years. Purchaser agrees to make formal application for loan within three business days from acceptance and further agrees to proceed in good faith to secure the loan." You would want guidance from your attorney on the specific wording of any contingency, including this one. You want to eliminate wiggle room.

Some wheeler and dealer buyers make offers to purchase on a number of properties at the same time and include contingencies that would permit them to walk away from any of them at their leisure. That gives them the ability to tie up a property while they sort through their options to decide which, if any, they actually want to purchase.

Appraisal. If the buyer wants to get a loan, the lender will insist that the property is worth what's being paid for it and will require a formal appraisal, paid for by the buyer (unless you volunteer to pay it). The lender will select the appraiser. If your agreed-upon selling price is $200,000 and the buyer is going to put down $20,000, the bank can be pretty certain that if the property is appraised at $200,000 there will be a good cushion with which to work in the event of the worst case—default and foreclosure.

What can go wrong with appraisals? The most obvious problem would arise if the property didn't "appraise out." If the appraiser's formal estimate of value were $190,000, the buyer would be off the hook. You can avoid losing your deal by going through the steps outlined in Chapter 8. A formal appraisal ahead of time by a professional appraiser would help to prevent any unpleasant surprises. Most sellers do not take this extra step, relying instead on information from other sources. If those other sources are reliable, it generally works out well.

Inspections. The appraiser will, in essence, perform a type of inspection, although the primary objective will be to arrive at an opinion of value. If there's a major observable flaw it will be noted and it will have to be corrected prior to the lender approving the loan, but it's a number the appraiser is after—what's it worth in dollars on the open market? Formal inspections go well beyond valuation and can include a variety of things. At times one inspector will perform all the tasks; at other times, several separate inspections can take place.

If you've already had a formal inspection and have the report available, along with a record of your corrective actions, it will quite likely satisfy the buyer. Even though having a formal inspection is an extremely effective marketing strategy, most sellers wait to see if they get an offer in which the buyers include an inspection as a contingency, as is increasingly common.

The difficulty arises when problems are found. How much will it cost to replace that faulty hot-water heater? Who pays? It is common for the inspection contingency to contain an agreed-upon total amount that would be the seller's responsibility. For example: "Seller agrees to reimburse buyer a maximum of $1,500 for items identified as in need of repair or replacement by a home inspection conducted by a state certified and bonded inspector and paid for by the buyer." What happens if it is discovered that a major repair is needed that would easily exceed the limit? You can see why it's better to find problems before you list and either correct them or discount your price.

Condition of Property at Close.   We will assume that when you put your home on the market you (or someone else) will still be living in it. The buyers will look it over when they are house hunting and they will make certain judgments. They will assume that the property will be in the same general configuration on closing day as it was when they originally looked at it. To insure that sellers maintain the condition of the house, some offers will contain a standard phrase such as, "Property will be delivered in broom clean condition." To guarantee that, a final-walk through by the buyers or their representative just prior to close is sometimes listed as a contingency.

As a seller I would hope that this were not a requirement, because it would provide buyers with a major weapon at a crucial time. If they were looking for leverage to get a last-minute concession, this phrase could give it to them. That's another reason you need to be attentive to signals about buyers' stability and character. Are they likely to be reasonable? On the other hand, if I were a buyer, I would want that option, because some sellers are not as honest and thoughtful as one would hope and could leave the place in a shambles. The bottom line is that I would hope that the contingency were not there, but I would not object if it were.

Sale of Buyer's Home.   Real estate professionals usually advise homeowners to sell first, then buy. Otherwise, the situation can become complicated. Should you accept an offer that contains a clause that reads something like, "Contingent upon purchaser's closing on the sale of their home at 79 Wistful Lane in Hilmar, California." It all depends. What are your other options? If your home has been on the market for an extended period and that's the only offer you've received or you think you're likely to receive, then it could be worth pursuing. I guess what I'm saying is that this kind of offer is probably better than nothing—but not much.

If you do agree to this contingency, make certain that you or your agent (if you have one) investigate thoroughly. Some people make offers without having even gone to the trouble of finding out how much their home is worth. Others may have had it listed for six months with no takers. Still others could have a sale pending and about to close. The real problem with agreeing to this contingency is that all of the leverage is with the buyer, and if you take your home off the market you've made a big gamble on an iffy situation.

Approval by a Third Party.   You may encounter this contingency when younger buyers want their parents to look over their selection or vice versa. The third party is often supplying part of the money for the purchase, so it can be a serious contingency. If the buyers impressed me as serious, responsible individuals I would not have too big a problem with this stipulation. I would insist on getting the third party's approval in a very short time, however. In working with buyers it is wise to work in this question as early in your relationship as possible: "Will anyone else be participating in your decision with you?"

Crunch Time

You've accepted an offer, the contingencies have been removed and there's one final hurdle to clear before you head into the sunset with that obscenely large check. It's called, among other things, settlement, closing, judgment day, the final reckoning or tally time. Whatever it's called, it's when the entire process comes together, and it's our last major subject.

Red Flag Checklist and Survival Strategies

1.   *A good friend learns that your home is on the market and says she wants to buy it from you. She makes a full-price written offer with terms that seem entirely reasonable. Your enthusiastic mate says, "We've both known Hilda since the second grade. Why don't we just go ahead and accept and save the money it would cost us to have this reviewed by an attorney."*

Strategy: Just to make absolutely certain that we understand each other or this point, let's assume your mother wants to buy your home. Your response? "Great, Mom, but to be sure that your interests are protected, let's run it by an attorney."

2.   *You have listed your home for $175,000 with a respected broker in town. Almost immediately he comes in with an offer for $125,000. He's apologetic but says the law requires him to present the offer to you.*

Strategy: This is what is known in the business as a lowball offer. The broker is correct: he must present any written offer he receives. The major problem with a lowball offer is that sellers typically get insulted. Keep your cool, don't be offended, and make a written counteroffer that's acceptable to you. It will only take a few minutes of your time and won't cost you anything. I have seen some people who make ridiculously low initial offers turn out eventually to be solid buyers. Not often, but it does happen.

3.   *As part of the purchase price for your home, the buyer offers you his vintage Rolls Royce.*

Strategy: Personal property is an acceptable form of consideration, presuming both buyer and seller agree. Assuming that owning this car appeals to you, your first step would be to get an independent appraisal of its actual value and verification that the buyer had good and unencumbered title. As a general rule, I advise against getting personal and real property mixed up in the same transaction. Lenders also don't generally like to see you (read "won't let you") mix them.

4. You are selling your home on your own and receive an offer to purchase accompanied by a personal check for $5,000 as an earnest money deposit. It is May 29 and the check is dated June 1. The buyer says that an automatic deposit will be made on June 1 that will adequately cover the check.

Strategy: We've probably all been in the position where we would have liked to postdate a check. It's a dangerous practice. First, if you do so and the person who receives it tries to cash it immediately, it could bounce. There's really no assurance a postdated check will be good until you actually present it for payment. I wouldn't rule it out automatically, but I would make it clear to the buyers that we didn't have a deal until the check cleared.

5. You receive an offer to purchase that looks great from buyers who look too good to be true. You make only one minor change on the offer—they want the drapes in the nursery to stay and you want to take them with you.

Strategy: I've seen solid transactions involving qualified buyers and sincere sellers fall apart over what, in retrospect, were incredibly minor issues. Just buy new drapes with all the money you will make. Changing anything on the offer would likely be construed as a counteroffer and relieve those too-good-to-be-true buyers from any further responsibility.

6. Within three days of listing your property you get what looks like a decent offer—actually more than you were expecting. However, the offer came in so quickly that you are tempted to wait to see what other responses you get.

Strategy: It is not at all uncommon for the first offers to be the best ones—sometimes the only ones. That's particularly true when you list with a broker and it goes on MLS. Every agent working with a buyer with a potential interest in your home will hustle to check it out. If you've done your homework and are satisfied that you've priced your home fairly, think carefully about turning down a good offer—even if it comes in almost immediately.

7. Your real estate agent brings you an offer with a contingency that the buyers sell their home first. He says he has looked at their house and he feels it would be readily marketable. He recommends you accept but that you continue to take back-up offers.

Strategy: Would you make an offer on a home that had a deal pending that would result in yours being a back-up offer? Most people want to get on with their lives. If I really needed to buy a home, I would move on to other options. A lot of other potential buyers will do the same thing.

8.   *After prolonged discussion, you and your spouse decide to sell your empty nest, even though the emotional ties are strong. Almost immediately you get a full-price offer from qualified buyers who are anxious to close the deal and move in. As you and your mate are considering the formal offer to purchase you say, almost in unison, "I don't want to sell!"*

Strategy: If you are selling on your own and have not formally accepted the offer, then you can exercise your prerogative to change your mind. You'll likely have some ticked-off buyers, but that's better than remorseful sellers. But if you've listed your home, the broker has produced that ready, willing and able buyer and has probably earned the commission. The moral: think hard before you decide to sell and harder before you list it.

9.   *You receive an offer to purchase with no requirement for a final walk-through inspection just prior to close.*

Strategy: Do not be lulled into a false sense of security. You would still be well advised to get the home as clean as possible. If buyers move in the day after close and find what they think is an unacceptable condition, they could still cause you legal difficulties, even if it were nothing more than a small-claims-court action.

10.   *After an initial surge of interest in your listing, several weeks pass with no offers. Then, incredibly, your real estate agent brings you three at one time.*

Strategy: On the surface, this "problem" looks easy—pick the highest offer. This option may indeed be correct; however, you should look at the potential buyers very carefully. If you are working with a real estate agent, the initial screening will have been done for you. I would also consider each buyer's motivation. The stronger the need to get located in a home in a short period (school starts in September) the more enthused they are apt to be about getting financing and about completing all the other preclose items promptly. In the best of all worlds, the most motivated will also have made the best offer.

12

·····▼·····

Judgment Day

In the immortal words of baseball bard Yogi Berra, "It ain't over till it's over." Nowhere could that admonition be better applied than to a real estate transaction. Until money changes hands and the deed to the property is delivered, it's still the bottom of the ninth. There are no victory celebrations until the last out is made.

The Main Event

What you will encounter at the actual closing will depend upon where you live, because customs vary widely. Although the specific procedures will differ, the basic essentials are the same. You show up with the keys to your home and leave with a lot of money. Actually, you get the check shortly after the closing takes place and the appropriate documents are recorded, but that will just give you some time to bask in the anticipation of admiring that long string of numbers you're going to see after the dollar sign on your check.

Lawyers' Heaven

In many places, attorneys are mainstays in real estate transactions, and when you close you will likely sit around a table with the buyers and their lawyer as well as your legal representative. Real estate agents and/or lender representatives may even be on hand. With all the people who need to sign the papers and their legal eagles on hand, as well as an assorted array of other cast members, it can be a fun group. It can also be very intimidating—profitable, but intimidating.

All about Escrow

In a large number of states, particularly in the western United States, the closing process is conducted primarily through escrow, a process in which money and documents are held by a neutral third party, called a stakeholder. The escrow agent represents both parties in the transaction (in essence a disclosed dual agent) and is responsible for accomplishing the myriad of tasks that must be performed to translate the original sales contract into a done deal. Escrow functions are typically regulated by a state agency that requires licensing and bonding. Escrow companies, title companies and lending institutions offer escrow services. You will quite frequently find escrow and title companies operating under one roof as a combined business.

Escrow closings can be friendly, comparatively informal affairs. Buyers and sellers generally attend separate meetings, and although attorneys are sometimes present, the only people sitting around the table may be the escrow agent and the sellers or the buyers and their real estate agents, if any. All of my experience as a practicing real estate agent has been in a state where escrow companies handle almost all of the closings. For that reason, and because my experience with them has been universally positive, you may detect a slight bias on my part. Most real estate licensees, by the way, become attached to specific escrow agents, because how well they do their job will determine how smoothly the transactions close and commission checks get issued.

If you are in an area where escrow companies operate and you are selling on your own, you need to establish early contact with a knowledgeable and helpful escrow agent, called a closer in some places, as well as with a title company representative. If you want to do some reading up on the subject, I recommend Sandy Gadow's book, *All About Escrow.*

Getting There

When you sell your home, an incredible number of things will have to be accomplished between the time you accept the seller's offer and that blissful day when it all comes together for what is fondly known as the final payout. Whether done by an attorney, an escrow agent, a real estate broker or you, here are some of the tasks.

Title

When you convey title to your property, you do so by giving the buyer a deed. Most deed forms require you to state that there are no liens, loans or other easements on the property other than the ones you disclose. To make certain that the essential facts relating to your property are known, an examination of title will be done. That title search will be conducted by either an attorney or a representative of a title company. If there is a lender or an informed buyer involved, title insurance will be required by both of them. Custom in many places is for the seller to pay for a standard title insurance policy for the buyer and for the buyer to pay for the title insurance for the lender.

No matter who pays, the original title search must take place. There is no law that says title insurance must be issued, but financing will not be possible without it. Insurance simply covers the title against loss for a specific set of circumstances. As record searches have become automated, this process has become more efficient. Once the investigation is done and everyone is satisfied, the actual deed will be prepared for your signature.

Financing

The buyer is primarily affected by this issue, but unless the process runs smoothly, there will be no mortgage money and no close. When an escrow company is involved, immediately after escrow is opened, the closing agent will contact the responsible loan processor to determine what requirements must be met before the lending institution will disburse funds for the mortgage. These requirements will include appraisals, credit checks, employment verification, inspections, certificates and dozens of other details.

Real estate agents will provide a lot of help in this area. Ensuring that buyers make a formal loan application and finish the process is a task that a conscientious real estate agent will put at the top of the "to do" list each day. If you are a fizzbo then I suggest you establish as good a rapport as possible with your buyers and check frequently with them to find out how the loan process is going.

Proration

The concept of proration is simple enough, but it can become extremely complicated in practice, and because money is involved, all participants are extremely interested in the end result.

Homeowners pay for a number of ongoing expenses. Among the most notable are property taxes, hazard insurance premiums, monthly homeowners' fees on condos, interest on loans and impound accounts. Some of these expenses are paid in advance, others in arrears. Someone has to tally debits and credits and arrive at a final settlement statement to determine who owes what to whom. The settlement date is the official dividing point. A brief illustration may help. If you have paid property taxes through June 30 and the transaction closes on June 1, then the buyers will live in the property for a month for which you have already paid the tab. Fairness dictates that they reimburse you at close for the appropriate amount. The person doing the prorating would determine the per-day amount and multiply it by the number of days and list it on your closing statement as a credit and on the buyer's closing statement as a debit.

Impound accounts (the payments you make each month so that the lending institution can pay your property taxes and hazard insurance when they are due) can be particularly confusing and can cause a great deal of consternation. They can accumulate a sizable amount of money, and the debits and credits must be accurately tabulated and explained to everyone's satisfaction. If you have an escrow agent or an experienced attorney, your only challenge will be to spend the time you need to make sure the basic calculations are correct. If for some reason the task is left up to you, beat a hasty retreat to your accountant.

Bottom Line Time

If the buyer of your home is getting financing from a lending institution, there will probably be a HUD-mandated standardized Uniform Settlement Statement (HUD Form 1) that reflects all the closing information, including buyer and seller charges and credits. There are frequently expenses for both buyer and seller that are paid outside of escrow and not required by the lender that will not appear on the form.

Even though you will be concerned primarily with the pluses and minuses as they relate to you, the seller, it's always a good idea to know what's going on with the buyer as well, particularly if you do not have a real estate agent involved.

Buyer Tally: Debits

These are examples of typical buyer debits on the HUD Form 1.

Purchase Price. This is the total amount of the purchase and will be the number from which credits are subtracted. It's the big number under the section "Gross Amount Due from Borrower."

Settlement Charges. Exactly how this number breaks out will depend upon how the closing is handled. Here are common charges.

- *Escrow fee.* This charge applies only if you close in escrow. Who pays is negotiable, although certain government-sponsored loans may impose restrictions on the amount the buyer may pay. The escrow fee is usually split evenly between buyer and seller, although in some places sellers customarily pay the entire amount. If I lived in an area like that and were a seller, I believe I would do some negotiating, although in the context of the total transaction, this is not a lot of money (perhaps $400 to $500 on a $150,000 to $200,000 house).

- *Attorney's fee.* Of course a buyer could have an attorney fee in any transaction, but if an attorney performs the closing functions in addition to routine guidance, the tab will be higher. I should mention in passing that even who pays the buyer's attorney is negotiable. If you want to do it, that's fine, although it's rarely done. The attorney will still represent the buyer.

- *Loan fees.* The prevailing philosophy is that costs associated with getting a loan are the responsibility of the purchasers, but as with most other items, it is negotiable. Loan origination fees, loan discount points, appraisal fees and credit report charges are examples of areas open to debate. If, in the context of the greater transaction, it seems to make sense to pay part of the buyer's loan costs, that is certainly allowable and perhaps even a good strategy.

- *Lender's title insurance.* This insurance covers the lender against possible claims against the title that could surface after the transaction closes. It's for the amount of the loan and the face amount decreases as the loan is paid off.

- *Hazard insurance.* In some instances, the seller's policy may be assumed by the buyer, but a completely new policy is more commonly obtained. If the buyer were to assume your policy, then you would be owed a rebate for the period you've already paid. The buyer will have to produce proof of insurance prior to close. I recommend that you cancel your insurance policy and get your rebate directly from your company. The buyers should get their own insurance.

- *Prorations.* As explained above, prorations will depend on the specific nature of the transaction and the status of various accounts, such as property tax and impounds.

- *Inspections.* It is probably most common for the buyer to order and pay for pest and dry rot and other inspections.

- *Recording fees.* These fees will involve documents such as the new deed.

Buyer Tally: Credits

Deposits.   This is the amount of any earnest-money deposit along with any additional deposit made prior to close.

Loans.   This is characteristically the largest credit to the buyer. If the price of the property is $125,000, the loan is for $100,000, and the earnest money and additional deposits $15,000, the buyer would need to come up with another $10,000 (plus other costs) at close.

Prorations.   Getting a credit at close for a proration on something like property tax will help the buyer's immediate cash position, but it will result in a payment being due somewhere down the line.

Seller Tally: Debits

Old Loan Payoffs.   If you have loans on your home, they must either be paid off or assumed. When there's a loan payoff, the amount paid will include interest up to the settlement date. Any prepayment penalty will be included, although it might not be listed as a separate item. Ask specifically and check the figures carefully.

Settlement Charges.　As was the case with the buyer, these fees will vary depending on the nature of the transaction.

- *Sales commission.* The loan payoff is generally the largest single seller debit, followed by the commission (although if you're a fizzbo there will be a nice blank space here). The amount of money paid to the real estate broker can be shocking, particularly when the sale was quick and painless. Some sellers have even been known to attempt to have the broker lower the fee at this point. You should make peace early on with the idea of paying what could be a five-figure commission. If you can't resign yourself to paying the agreed upon amount if the services are delivered, avoid the whole problem by selling without a broker.

- *Transfer tax.* These taxes can amount to quite a lot, depending on where you live. Many places have no real property transfer taxes, but they are becoming more prevalent.

- *Escrow fees.* If you close in escrow you will know early on what this charge will be, because who pays what will have been settled in the offer to purchase and the escrow company can give you an exact figure. The fee will depend partly on the sales price.

- *Attorney fees.* You can pay your attorney fees outside of closing or have them included. Some people who have not previously worked with attorneys are surprised to learn that in most instances even a telephone call asking for advice will result in a charge. Don't be shy—discuss charges ahead of time.

- *Prorations.* Prorations can be quite substantial in some instances, and sellers are often surprised. You shouldn't be if you've been properly counseled about what to expect and about the rationale behind the process. The good news is that it's money you won't get as opposed to money you must pay.

Seller Tally: Credits

Now for the fun part. It's short but sweet.

Sales Price.   This is the big one. Assuming it's large enough to cover all those debits and leave you with a nice little "due seller at close," everything else becomes a lot more bearable.

Prorations.   You could even get a few dollars here for money that you previously parted with.

Moving On

Self-confidence is a wonderful thing. Whether completely on your own or with the help of a real estate agent, selling your home is a worthy challenge. Once you've done it successfully, and profitably, it will likely embolden you to seek out other challenges in the wonderful world of real estate. The next chapter will contain some final thoughts and suggestions.

Red Flag Checklist and Survival Strategies

1.   The real estate agent with whom you are working tells you that her broker can handle the closing process and recommends that you use his services.

Strategy: In some states real estate brokers are permitted to handle closings, but I would much prefer a completely independent closing agent. You want your interests represented in the best possible fashion without the slightest possibility of a conflict of interest. It's hard for me to see how a broker who will get a commission could qualify as a disinterested third party.

2.   When you bought your home several years ago, the owner took back the mortgage, so there was no lender involved. You do not recall having received a title insurance policy.

Strategy: Lack of title insurance could signal real problems if there are clouds on the title that were not revealed to you as a result of a formal title search. Such problems are unlikely to arise, but you need assurance, which is why it's critical to get a preliminary title report early in your homeselling project.

3.   *As a fizzbo you know it's important to keep checking with your buyers to insure that the loan process is going well, but you keep getting evasive answers when you ask them about their progress.*

Strategy: Even if your buyers have satisfied the requirement to apply for a loan, that's just the first step. I would insist on concrete evidence that all was progressing on track. Ask them where they have applied and for the name of their loan processor. If I were concerned, I would call that person and ask if there was anything I could do to help expedite matters. If I got bad vibes then I would call for a summit meeting with the buyers to either get things on track or bail out.

4.   *Your property is in the country with a large, irregularly shaped lot. To your knowledge there has not been a formal survey done since the original development many years ago.*

Strategy: The standard form of title insurance does not cover anything that would be discovered by a formal survey. As an example, if there were an encroachment problem (your neighbor built a fence on your property), that might cloud the title and would not be covered. An astute buyer may insist upon a formal survey both for peace of mind and for title insurance purposes. Who pays for it would be subject to negotiation.

5.   *You have sold your home on your own to a young couple who are buying their first home. They are well qualified and their loan was approved quickly. As you approach formal close they start calling and asking questions that seem to reflect an unusual degree of anxiety.*

Strategy: It is not at all unusual for "buyer's remorse" to strike any homebuyer, but first-timers seem particularly susceptible. Calm reassurance is the best antidote. It's also possible they may not understand the closing process completely, so it would be wise to check with your closer to see if you can ferret out any possible sources of misunderstanding.

6.   When you received an offer on your home, your were given a "seller's net" estimate from your real estate agent. It reflected the amount of money you were projected to clear at close. When you review closing documents it turns out you will net significantly less.

Strategy: An experienced real estate agent will be able to come close to estimating your net proceeds, but some variables in certain transactions are difficult to pinpoint, and unforseen expenses occasionally arise. However, both you and the agent should be working with the closing official to make certain that you are aware of any major deviations. Mistakes sometimes occur. On rare occasions some real estate agents have been known to overestimate net proceeds to encourage a seller to accept an offer. It's good to be well informed early, stay on top of the situation and ask a lot of questions.

7.   An acquaintance of yours, not known for his honesty or integrity, is aware that you will be making a tidy profit on the sale of your home. "What a windfall," he volunteers. "Because that's not earned income, the IRS will never know about it."

Strategy: As you might suspect, the IRS has long since plugged that loophole to remove any temptation folks might have to inadvertently forget to report their capital gain to Uncle Sam. Every real estate transaction must be reported to the IRS by the closing agent on Form 1099-S. The sales price and the amount of property tax reimbursement as well as the seller's social security number must be provided.

8.   When you review your settlement statement prior to close, you are confused by an expense identified as a buyer's credit and seller's debit for interest on your mortgage loan, which is being assumed.

Strategy: When you make your mortgage payment each month, you pay the interest in arrears—that is, for the preceding month. For example, the June 1 payment will include interest for the month of May. Therefore, if the buyers assume your loan on May 31 and make the payment on June 1, they will have paid for time you occupied the property and should be reimbursed at close.

9.   You are closing in escrow and have heard that you are entitled to review official closing documents (the HUD Form 1) one business day before closing.

You call your escrow agent and are informed that you do not have that right—
it applies only to borrowers.

Strategy: I would be nervous. Technically, the Real Estate Settlement Procedures Act (RESPA) provides only borrowers with this right, but I can't imagine why an escrow agent would not agree to share them with a seller. I would definitely consider this a red flag and trot on over to my attorney's office.

10.   *You have been assured that a prepayment penalty on your second mortgage will not be charged to you because your buyer is getting a loan at the same lending institution. However, when you see your closing statement, the payoff figure for the loan looks excessive.*

Strategy: Sometimes breakdowns in communications occur. When I refinanced my home, I paid off a second mortgage with a prepayment penalty. I was assured that because I was refinancing with the same bank I would not be charged that prepayment fee. I was, although it was included in the total payoff and not listed separately. The bank manager stepped in and straightened it out, but if I had not known the amount of my mortgage balance and what to look for, I would have paid it without knowing.

13

·····▼·····

On the Road Again

For many people, the time they have to sit back and contemplate their glorious and profitable homeselling victory is fleeting. They must immediately change hats and become homebuyers instead of homesellers. If that's your situation here are some final suggestions on how to best make that transition. You should also be on the alert for some other intriguing possibilities.

Strange thoughts sometimes begin to enter the minds of people who have recently participated in a successful real estate transaction. Things like, "Gee, that was so much fun I think I might like to do it for a living." Or, "Wow, we did so well, why don't we start investing in real estate by getting a rental property?" Just in case you've been having such thoughts, we'll also provide some general guidance.

Homebuyer Survival Strategies

If buying another home is next on your immediate agenda, you will be well prepared because of your recent, successful experience in the real estate marketplace. However, it would be wise to hone your skills and make certain you are completely up to date.

Do Your Homework

This is the major difference between selling a home and buying one. When you buy one, you are left to live with—and in—the end result of the whole process. Make a mistake and it could be years of regret, not to mention financial heartache. The vast majority of real estate lawsuits are filed by disgruntled homebuyers.

You should shift the focus of your research efforts and start reading some books devoted to homebuying. The bibliography contains a list of several good ones. You will note there is one entitled *The Homebuyer's Survival Guide,* which should be particularly helpful to you in establishing an overall homebuying strategy and assist you in avoiding serious problems. The fact that I wrote it naturally has nothing to do with my recommendation.

Deep in the Heart of Taxes

No matter how much we wish, we cannot relegate tax matters to the back burner after selling a home. If you own or plan to acquire any real property, taxes demand your constant attention, or you could end up paying big money. It's critical that you be well informed, keep good records, stay current and retain competent professional help. There are several excellent consumer periodicals that will help you stay abreast of what's happening in business and investment matters, including real estate and income tax. *Money* and *Kiplinger's Personal Finance* are two of the most informative publications and can be found in almost all libraries. Before you start your homebuying quest, you should browse through the last half dozen issues or so of each.

Check Out the Local Scene

If you plan to buy another home near the one you've just sold, you already know the local housing situation. You will be particularly in tune with market values and will be able to recognize well priced (and overpriced) homes when you see them. If, however, you are heading for distant places, you should become completely familiar with the ground rules there—most particularly prices.

When I actively sold real estate in Oregon I worked extensively with buyers who were relocating from California, where home prices were in another galaxy. The reaction was typically stunned disbelief when you informed them of the price of a particular piece of property. I just loved working with those equity-rich folks. If, where you are going, you can buy a small farm for what you got for your little

800-square-foot bungalow, that doesn't necessarily mean that the small farm you are looking at is priced right. And, unfortunately, you might be moving from the lower-priced area to the higher one, which can cause lots of problems. Get plugged in as soon as possible to the market where you are going—not where you are coming from.

Rely On a REALTOR®

I have to admit that when *selling* your home there are some pretty good arguments for going the Fizzbo route. On the other hand, when you're buying, I strongly recommend you find a REALTOR® whom you trust and with whom you are compatible and work exclusively with her or him or them (some work in teams). It will save you time and energy and will most likely insure you get the best house for the least money and the fewest hassles.

There are some cautions, however. First, I would not sign a buyer broker contract. Depending upon where you buy, you may be asked to acknowledge that you understand the agency relationship in the transaction, and that's fine. I would not go beyond that. I would never agree in writing to work with one buyer agent exclusively, although it would be my intent to do just that. I would simply want the freedom to change my mind without obligation. It is quite probable that you can find a REALTOR® to represent you as a buyer's agent with the fee to come from the transaction, which means from the commission the seller is paying.

If you find the unquestioned home of your dreams and the owner is a steely eyed, grumpy Fizzbo who will not consent under any circumstances to have a real estate agent involved in the transaction, you will have to proceed on your own. Because of your experience, that shouldn't pose a big problem for you, and you would still have your attorney in your corner.

Deal from a Position of Strength

It makes no difference whether it's a buyer's market or a seller's market, a well-qualified buyer is always the most coveted prize in the homebuying/homeselling process. We'll assume that you stashed away a portion of that nice check you received at closing for your down payment and closing costs (remember, when the final debit/credit tally is completed on judgment day, the buyer has to come up with a sizable amount of cash) and that your credit rating remains impeccable.

I recommend you get preapproval for a loan (not just prequalification) before you start looking for a home. With your assets, you'll be a hot commodity, and with your knowledge, it will be apparent to all that you are to be taken seriously.

A Career in Real Estate?

When the air force moved us from Alabama to Oregon, we sold our home ourselves. My wife and I thoroughly enjoyed the experience, and it saved us almost $4,000 (that's when you could buy a comfortable four-bedroom, three-bath home in Montgomery for $60,000). I'm pretty sure that experience planted the idea of a real estate career in both our minds. It's a great profession if you're suited for it, particularly if you've got a salaried spouse with a job that has good benefits. It even has possibilities as a part-time career or as a means of locating good investment opportunities for yourself. There are strict disclosure requirements and other consumer safeguards, but there's no law against a licensed agent buying investment real estate.

A License To Sell

To sell real estate that doesn't belong to you, you must be licensed, which means passing a written, objective test administered by a state agency. In most states you must also attend formal classroom training. It's definitely not easy, but it's an entirely achievable objective if you persevere a little.

Consumer Alert

Even if you're not terribly interested in getting your license, I highly recommend the coursework for your general education. In the three-course prelicensing sequence that I teach in the adult division of the local community college, about 20 to 30 percent of the students are typically there just to become more informed consumers and investors. Although some of what you will learn will be of primarily academic interest, a great deal of it will be extremely practical and immediately useful.

Getting the Word

My first major writing project after I began selling real estate was a book called *Your Successful Real Estate Career.* One publisher turned it down with the comment, "I really doubt there's a market for an honest book about selling real estate." Fortunately the American Management Association disagreed, it's now in its second edition and is the all-time best selling-real estate career guide written for the general public. I wrote it for people who want a hype-free assessment of the opportunities as well as the challenges of a real estate career. There's a lot of both. As one reviewer put it: "*Your Successful Real Estate Career* portrays the work just as it is, hemorrhoids and all."

Landlording Redux

You know from my comments in Chapter 1 that I think owning residential rental property makes a lot of sense for some people. Whether you are one of those people has a lot to do with your temperament and financial capability. If you have an extra few thousand kicking around after you sell your house that you don't need to buy another one, that would be a logical time to take a hard look at possible investment opportunities.

When you enter this arena you need specialized help. Find a REALTOR® who has experience in locating small investment properties and who can give you an initial estimate of potential cash flows. Before you make an offer on any property, insist on seeing that portion of the seller's federal income tax statements where the history of the property is reported. On tax returns, sellers report all possible expenses and are conservative in stating actual income. If your accountant does not have experience in this area, you should consider moving on to someone who does.

Talk to other people who have been down the same path and get their recommendations for real estate professionals, accountants and attorneys. Almost all cities of any size have a property management organization composed of people with similar interests. You can have serious difficulty if you inadvertently violate such things as fair-housing laws, so it's wise to be affiliated with a group whose purpose is to keep its members informed of recent developments and potential trouble areas. Make certain you also visit your insurance agent to satisfy yourself that you have adequate coverage, including liability.

Bon Voyage!

I hope your homeselling venture turns out to be both enjoyable and incredibly profitable. As we've seen, it could even open the door to possibilities you hadn't considered. Keep your eye on your goal, look out for number one and persevere. Good luck!

Appendix

———•———

State Real Estate Commissions

Alabama
Real Estate Commission
1201 Carmichael Way
Montgomery, AL 36106
(205) 242-5544

Alaska
Department of Occupational
Licensing
3601 C Street, Suite 722
Anchorage, AK 99503
(907) 563-2169

Arizona
Department of Real Estate
202 East Earll Drive, #400
Phoenix, AZ 85012-2623
(602) 279-2909

Arkansas
Real Estate Commission
612 Summit Street
Little Rock, AR 72201-4740
(501) 682-2732

California
Department of Real Estate
185 Berry Street, Room 3400
San Francisco, CA 94107
(415) 904-5900

Colorado
Real Estate Commission
1776 Logan Street, 4th Floor
Denver, CO 80203
(303) 894-2166

Connecticut
Real Estate Division
165 Capitol Avenue, Room G-8
Hartford, CT 06106
(203) 566-5130

Delaware
Department of Administrative
Services
P.O. Box 1401
Dover, DE 19902
(302) 739-4522

District of Columbia
Department of Consumer Affairs
614 H Street N.W., Room 913
P.O. Box 37200
Washington, DC 20013-7200
(202) 727-7853

Florida
Division of Real Estate
400 W. Robinson Street
Orlando, FL 32801
(407) 423-6053

Georgia
Real Estate Commission
Suite 500 - Sussex Place
148 International Boulevard N.E.
Atlanta, GA 30303-1734
(404) 656-3916

Hawaii
Real Estate Commission
250 S. King Street, Room 702
Honolulu, HI 96813
(808) 586-2643

Idaho
Real Estate Commission
Statehouse Mail
Boise, ID 83720
(208) 334-3285

Illinois
Department of Professional
Regulation
320 West Washington, 3rd Floor
Springfield, IL 62786
(217) 782-7566

Indiana
Professional Licensing Agency
1021 Government Center N
100 North Senate Avenue
Indianapolis, IN 46204
(317) 232-2980

Iowa
Real Estate Commission
1918 S. E. Hulsizer Road
Ankeny, IA 50021
(515) 281-3183

Kansas
Real Estate Commission
900 Jackson Street, Room 501
Topeka, KS 66612-1220
(913) 296-3411

Kentucky
Real Estate Commission
10200 Linn Station Road,
Suite 201
Louisville, KY 40233
(502) 425-4273

Louisiana
Real Estate Commission
P.O. Box 14785
Baton Rouge, LA 70898
(504) 925-4771

Maine
Real Estate Commission
State House Station #35
Augusta, ME 04333
(207) 582-8727

Maryland
Real Estate Commission
501 St. Paul Place, Suite 804
Baltimore, MD 21202
(410) 333-6230

Massachusetts
Real Estate Board
100 Cambridge Street, Room 1518
Boston, MA 02202
(617) 727-2373

Michigan
Department of Commerce
P.O. Box 30243
Lansing, MI 48909
(517) 373-0490

Minnesota
Department of Commerce
133 East 7th Street
St. Paul, MN 55101
(612) 296-2488

Mississippi
Real Estate Commission
1920 Dunbarton Drive
Jackson, MS 39216-5087
(601) 987-3969

Missouri
Real Estate Commission
P.O. Box 1339
Jefferson City, MO 65102
(314) 751-2628

Montana
Board of Realty Regulation
Arcade Building
111 North Jackson
Helena, MT 59620
(406) 444-2961

Nebraska
Real Estate Commission
P.O. Box 94667
Lincoln, NE 68509
(402) 471-2004

Nevada
Real Estate Division
1665 Hot Springs Road
Carson City, NV 89710
(702) 687-4280

New Hampshire
Real Estate Commission
95 Pleasant Street
Concord, NH 03301
(603) 271-2701

New Jersey
Real Estate Commission
20 West State Street
Trenton, NJ 08625
(609) 292-8280

New Mexico
Real Estate Commission
1650 University Blvd N.E.,
    Suite 490
Albuquerque, NM 87102
(505) 841-9120

New York
Division of Licensing
162 Washington Avenue
Albany, NY 12231
(518) 486-6451

North Carolina
Real Estate Commission
P.O. Box 17100
Raleigh, NC 27619-7100
(919) 733-9580

North Dakota
Real Estate Commission
P.O. Box 727
Bismarck, ND 58502
(701) 224-2749

Ohio
Division of Real Estate
77 South High Street, 20th Floor
Columbus, OH 43266-0547
(614) 466-4100

Oklahoma
Real Estate Commission
4040 North Lincoln Boulevard,
    Suite 100
Oklahoma City, OK 73105
(405) 521-3387

Oregon
Real Estate Agency
1177 Center Street N.E.
Salem, OR 97310-2503
(503) 378-4170

Pennsylvania
Real Estate Commission
P.O. Box 2649
Harrisburg, PA 17105-2649
(717) 783-3658

Rhode Island
Real Estate Division
233 Richmond Street
Providence, RI 02903
(401) 277-2255

South Carolina
Real Estate Commission
1201 Main Street, Suite 1500
Columbia, SC 29201
(803) 737-0700

South Dakota
Real Estate Commission
P.O. Box 490
Pierre, SD 57501
(605) 773-3600

Tennessee
Real Estate Commission
500 James Robertson Parkway
Suite 180, Volunteer Plaza
Nashville, TN 37243-1151
(615) 741-2273

Texas
Real Estate Commission
P.O. Box 12188
Austin, TX 78711-2188
(512) 459-6544

Utah
Division of Real Estate
P.O. Box 45806
Salt Lake City, UT 84145
(801) 530-6747

Vermont
Real Estate Commission
109 State Street
Montpelier, VT 05609
(802) 828-3228

Virginia
Department of Commerce
3600 West Broad Street, 5th Floor
Richmond, VA 23230
(804) 367-8552

Washington
Real Estate Division
P.O. Box 9015
Olympia, WA 98507
(206) 586-6101

West Virginia
Real Estate Commission
1033 Quarrier Street, Suite 400
Charleston, WV 25301
(304) 348-3555

Wisconsin
Real Estate Bureau
P.O. Box 8935
Madison, WI 53708
(608) 267-7134

Wyoming
Real Estate Commission
205 Barrett Building
Cheyenne, WY 82002
(307) 777-7141

Source: Association of Real Estate License Law Officials (ARELLO), P.O. Box 129, Centerville, UT 84014-0129.

Bibliography

Real Estate Reference

Arnold, Alvin L. *The Arnold Encyclopedia of Real Estate.* New York: John Wiley and Sons, 1993. A hard-cover heavyweight and an excellent basic resource.

Reilly, John W. *The Ultimate Language of Real Estate.* Chicago: Dearborn Financial Publishing, 1993. I refer to this reference, written by an attorney/real estate broker, more than any other.

Homeselling Reference

Bly, Amy Sprecher, and Robert W. Bly. *How To Sell Your House, Condo, Co-Op.* Yonkers, N.Y.: Consumer Reports Books, 1993.

Irwin, Robert. *Tips and Traps When Selling a Home.* New York: McGraw Hill, 1990. Irwin has written a "Tips and Traps" book on just about every subject relating to real estate. They're helpful.

Lank, Edith. *The Homeseller's Kit.* Chicago: Dearborn Financial Publishing, 1994. Lank writes the "House Calls" column for the Los Angeles Times Syndicate and is the author of several excellent books.

Miller, Peter G. *How To Sell Your Home in Any Market.* New York: Harper and Row, 1994. Miller's *Common Sense Mortgage* is his most popular work, but this book also contains excellent material.

Shenkman, Martin M., and Warren Boroson. *How To Sell Your House in a Buyer's Market.* New York: John Wiley, 1990. Shenkman is an attorney, so this book offers practical legal insights.

Homebuying Reference

Boroson, Warren, and Ken Austin. *The Home Buyer's Inspection Guide.* New York: John Wiley, 1993. Also helpful if you're selling.

Buying and Selling a Home. Washington, D.C.: Kiplinger Books, 1993. Prepared by the staff of *Kiplinger's Personal Finance Magazine,* this book contains an incredible amount of excellent resource material.

Edwards, Kenneth W. *The Homebuyer's Survival Guide.* Chicago: Dearborn Financial Publishing, 1994.

Fields, Alan, and Denise Fields. *Your New House.* Boulder, Colo.: Windsor Peak Press, 1993. Whether you're buying a new house or an old one, this is a good source.

Irwin, Robert. *Tips and Traps When Buying a Home.* New York: McGraw Hill, 1990.

Lank, Edith. *The Homebuyer's Kit.* Chicago: Dearborn Financial Publishing, 1994.

Reed, John. *Residential Property Acquisition Handbook.* Danville, Calif.: Reed Publishing, 1993.

Vila, Bob. *Bob Vila's Guide to Buying Your Dream House.* New York: Little Brown and Co., 1990.

Real Estate Law

Coit, Charles S. *Introduction to Real Estate Law.* Chicago: Dearborn Financial Publishing, 1989.

Cooper, Cynthia. *Homeowner's Legal Guide.* Yonkers, N.Y.: Consumer Reports Books, 1993.

Gibson, Frank, James Karp, and Elliot Klayman. *Real Estate Law.* Chicago: Dearborn Financial Publishing, 1992.

Kratovil, Robert, and Raymond J. Werner. *Real Estate Law.* Englewood Cliffs, N.J.: Prentice-Hall, 1988.

Real Estate and Taxes

Hoven, Vernon. *Real Estate Investor's Tax Guide.* Chicago: Dearborn Financial Publishing, 1993. Written by a CPA who specializes in real estate tax matters, this is an outstanding reference.

Lank, Edith, and Miriam Geisman. *Your Home as a Tax Shelter.* Chicago: Dearborn Financial Publishing, 1993. This book will tell you all you need to know about the tax advantages of home ownership.

Real Estate Finance

Dennis, Marshall W. *Residential Mortgage Lending.* Englewood Cliffs, N.J.: Prentice-Hall, 1992. This book, written by a banking insider, is an excellent basic reference.

Garton-Good, Julie. *All About Mortgages.* Chicago: Dearborn Financial Publishing, 1994. If you have a question on mortgages, the answer is here.

Miller, Peter G. *The Common Sense Mortgage.* New York: Harper Collins Publishers, 1994. This book has proved so popular that Miller revises it frequently.

Real Estate Property Management

Irwin, Robert. *The Landlord's Troubleshooter.* Chicago: Dearborn Financial Publishing, 1994. Good down-to-earth advice from the "tips and traps" man.

Kyle, Robert C., and Floyd M. Baird. *Property Management.* Chicago: Dearborn Financial Publishing, 1991. This is a basic textbook.

Reed, John T. *How To Manage Residential Property for Maximum Cash Flow and Resale Value.* Danville, Calif.: Reed Publishing, 1993. Reed is a no-nonsense real estate investor/educator/writer. He also publishes an informative newsletter. Information: 1-800-635-5425.

Robinson, Leigh. *Landlording.* El Cerrito, Calif.: ExPress, 1994. First published in 1975 and still going strong, this book provides as practical a hands-on treatment of the subject as you will find.

Real Estate Appraisal

Appraising Residential Properties. Chicago: American Institute of Real Estate Appraisers, 1988.

The Dictionary of Real Estate Appraisal. Chicago: The Appraisal Institute, 1993.

Real Estate Closings

Gadow, Sandy. *All About Escrow.* El Cerrito, Calif.: ExPress, 1992. An excellent book published by the same people who published *Landlording.*

Real Estate Careers

Edwards, Kenneth W. *Your Successful Real Estate Career.* New York: American Management Association, 1993.

Garton-Good, Julie. *SuperCourse for Real Estate Licensing.* New York: Simon and Schuster, 1990.

Kennedy, Danielle. *How to List and Sell Real Estate in the '90s.* Englewood Cliffs, N.J.: Prentice-Hall, 1990.

Reilly, John W., and Paige Bovee Vitousek. *Questions and Answers to Help You Pass the Real Estate Exam.* Chicago: Dearborn Financial Publishing, 1992.

Real Estate Videos

Knox, Dave. *Pricing Your Home to Sell.* Knox has other useful videos on home-buying and selling. Minneapolis, MN, 1992. Information: 1-800-533-1970.

Schwarz, Barb. *How to Prepare Your Home for Sale so It Sells!* Seattle, WA, 1992. Information: 1-800-392-7161.

Index

———————●———————